SPECIAL TEAMS– THE WINNING EDGE

Dick Arbuckle
Chuck Mottley

ISBN: 1-58518-311-3
Library of Congress Number: 2001098597

Book layout and cover design: Rebecca Gold Rubin, Jennifer Bokelmann

Coaches Choice
P.O. Box 1828
Monterey, CA 93942
www.coacheschoice.com

DEDICATION

To the best teammates in the world, my wife, Sherry, and our
three children, Vicki, Becki and Joe.

Dick Arbuckle

To my bride, Linda, a fan who learned to love football at Oklahoma University.

Chuck Mottley

ACKNOWLEDGMENTS

To the many coaches and players from whom I have had the opportunity to learn throughout my coaching career. There is a long held premise in coaching that there is really nothing new occurring in football. Rather, there is a recycling and repackaging of old concepts in an attempt to improve on them. I want to acknowledge that this is mostly what I have done in my experience as a coach. Much of the contents of this book represent knowledge and materials I have collected from many sources over a period of time. And, subsequently tried to improve upon them and add some uniqueness as time and experience has permitted.

I would be remiss if I didn't acknowledge the contributions of some of the most influential people on the realization of this book:

• My fellow co-author, Chuck Mottley, who encouraged me to undertake the writing of this book.

• Coach Gene Victor, my junior and senior high school coach in El Monte, California, for showing me how to train hard, reach high, and finish strong.

• Two head coaches, Don Read at the University of Oregon, and Bruce Snyder at Cal Berkeley and Arizona State University. They gave me the opportunity to coach the kicking game in addition to being a position coach. In both cases these men contributed a wealth of knowledge and encouraged me to be innovative in teaching the kicking game.

• Steve Mariucci, currently the head coach of the San Francisco Forty Niners, who was my predecessor as special teams coordinator at Cal Berkeley. Steve unselfishly gave me a tremendous amount of his time and expertise during the transition, even though he had a full plate as the offensive coordinator.

• NFL special teams coaches, Richard Smith, currently with the San Francisco Forty Niners, and Joe Marciano of the Tampa Bay Buccaneers. They have shared their cutting edge concepts with me and tolerated my "Curious George"-like questions with great patience.

• My mother, Dorothy Pyeatt Arbuckle, a single mom who sacrificed a great deal so that her youngest son could participate in sports and achieve a college education.

• And, the one person who stands out above all the rest, my wonderful wife, Sherry. Her encouragement and unwavering loyalty have enabled me to keep going in my chosen profession through all the good, as well as the challenging, times. I greatly appreciate her partnering with me in the only work I ever wanted to do.

I would also like to thank God for blessing me with a wonderful family, many true friends, and the opportunity to serve Him as a coach and teacher.

CONTENTS

Dick Arbuckle is and has been for 30 plus years one of the best special teams coaches in the country. Coach Arbuckle's expertise has been proven over and over again against countless opponents.

This individual's mastery of special teams has been reflective over the course of his coaching career not only in his use of sound creative technology, but with his ability to communicate this to his players. The "winning edge" that this extraordinary coach expounds upon in this book is exactly that! His insights to the kicking game are dissected far and beyond the norm.

Statistics, former players, fellow coaches and fans all continuously testify to the merits and know-how of Dick Arbuckle. The man is super organized and extremely motivated. As readers of this text, you and I would be hard pressed to identify any special teams coach, college or professional, that can compare to this man. He is truly special at what he does; provide the winning edge to the teams he coaches.

> Dan Read
> Football Coach Emeritus
> University of Montana

CHAPTER 1

PHILOSOPHY AND SCOPE OF THE KICKING GAME

The kicking game can provide the "winning edge" when every player and coach on the team wholeheartedly believes in its importance to the ultimate goal of "winning." There will be several games during a season in which big plays in the kicking game will directly determine who wins the contest. And, in all games, the kicking game usually has a substantial impact on the outcome of the game, either positively or negatively.

An examination of statistics reconfirm the importance of the kicking game. For example, between twenty to thirty percent of all plays in a game are kicking plays. Furthermore, approximately thirty percent of all points scored in a game come from special teams plays. In fact, there will be approximately ninety to one hundred big plays each season that involve special teams, either for or against. And, finally, large chunks of field position are gained or lost during kicking plays.

Head Coach Commitment

A real commitment is needed by the head coach to allocate practice time, coaching staff, and player meeting and practice time in order to realize success in the kicking game. There can be no doubt in the minds of the staff and players as to the importance of the kicking game.

Field Position

The *kicking game* gains importance when you realize how important a role it plays in determining a team's offensive scoring ability. The farther away an offense starts from its intended goal, the more difficult it will be to score. Conversely, the closer the offense starts, the easier it will be to score. The defensive field chart illustrated in Table 1-1 clearly shows this difference.

	Yard Line	Chances of Scoring
Own	20	1 out of 30
	40	1 out of 8
	50	1 out of 5
Opponent's	40	1 out of 3
	20	1 out of 2
	10	2 out of 3

Table 1-1. Relative chances of scoring depending on starting field position.

The significance of this information is simply that the kicking game can be utilized to give opponents poor scoring percentage and can enhance the offense's scoring percentages. For example, on kickoffs, if the opponent starts inside their own 20-yard line, their chances of scoring are quite *poor*. On punts, if a team can return to the 40-yard line or beyond, it greatly increases the offense's scoring ability.

Scope of the Kicking Game

The kicking game is comprised of many elements, including punt protection and coverage, fielding kicks, punt returns, punt blocks, field position consideration, P.A.T. and field-goal protection, P.A.T. and field-goal blocks, field- goal coverage and returns, fake kicks and fake kick defense, kickoff coverage and returns, onside kickoffs, and preparations for defending onside kickoffs. It also includes kicking tactics, strategy, fundamentals, sideline organization, and kicking game rules. To have a great kicking game, a team should be proficient in *all* of these areas.

There are three equally important elements of play in football—defense, offense, and kicking. As such, special teams should be given the same priority as the offense or defense. If not, the lack of appropriate emphasis on the kicking game will often show up on game day, usually in a negative way.

Something very unusual occurs on every kicking play in a game. One or more of the following three events that typically do not occur on other scrimmage plays takes place on every kicking play:

- A sizeable amount of yardage is involved (40 yards or more).
- There is a change of ball possession involved.
- A specific attempt to score points is involved. (P.A.T. or field goal attempt).

In a special-teams effort, points can also be scored in several ways:

- Safety
- Kickoff returns
- Punt returns
- Punt or field goal blocks for a score
- Recover a kickoff in end zone
- Advance fumbled kickoff or punt for a score
- Intercept a fake punt or field goal for a touchdown

Insofar as they affect the tide and outcome of the game, the plays involving the kicking game are weighted heavily .

Momentum

The momentum of a game can change on a great play in the kicking game. Many of the "big breaks" in a game occur on a kicking play. When a team is prepared, the chance to capitalize upon a break generally presents itself at a more opportune time. Not surprisingly, the kicking game often makes the difference between winning and losing.

Specialists

Kicking involves precise skills. The so-called "specialists" on the special teams, (i.e., punters, snappers, holders, place kickers, and returners), must work many extra hours at perfecting their skills. The distance at which kickers and holders locate themselves, along with the timing involved in snapping the ball and getting kicks away, must be worked on earnestly and tirelessly. Because these times and distance requirements are very precise, they require constant attention and concentration.

Timing

For best results and safety reasons, the following requirements can serve as performance guides for the three basic types of kicks in a game:

- Punts:

✓ The snap (15 yards)	0.7 to 0.8 seconds
✓ Punter (ball in hands time)	1.2 to 1.3 seconds
✓ Total get-off time	1.9 to 2.1 seconds
✓ Hang time	4.3 seconds-plus
✓ Punt coverage time	4.2-4.5 seconds hang (30-35 yards coverage); 4.8 seconds hang (40 yards coverage); 5.1 seconds hang (45 yards coverage)

- P.A.T. and field goal:

✓ Get-off time	1.3 seconds

- Kickoffs:

✓ Hang time	4.0 seconds (minimum)
✓ Distance	inside the 5-yard line

Special Teams Basic Outline

KICKOFF COVER TEAM

- *Objective.* To give the defense good field position by keeping the receiving team inside the 23-yard line. Create *quick turnovers. Intimidate* the opponent.

- *Specialist.* A kicker who kicks the ball to the goal line, and lofts it high enough to delay the return and allow the coverage to get down the field. He must also keep the kick *in-bounds*. (On an out-of-bounds kick, the rule allows the return team to take the ball on the 35-yard line, or, have the ball kicked over from the 30-yard line).

- *Team.* Fast, sure tacklers moving downfield, evenly spaced with a *burning desire to make the tackle.*

ONSIDE KICKOFF TEAM

- *Objective.* To recover a deliberate short kick. Gain great field position for the offense.

- *Specialist.* A kicker to dribble the ball a legal minimum of 10 yards. This technique must be perfected!

- *Team.* SWARM the recovery man and get the ball. All onside kicks must be recovered.

PUNT DEFENSE TEAM

- *Return objective.* To return each punt a minimum of 10 yards. To always give the offense good field position. Handle each punt properly. Net no more than 33 yards/punt.

- *Return specialist.* Quick, tricky punt returners who have sure hands and use their blockers. They must catch the ball (i.e., seldom let the ball hit the ground). Fair catches should be almost nonexistent when a return is called.

- *Team.* Fast, open-field blockers who use good judgment to avoid blocking illegally. Must stay onside and avoid *roughing the kicker.*

- *Block objective.* To block the punt, giving the punt defense team a touchdown or good field position. Always try to advance a blocked punt that hasn't crossed the L.O.S.

- *Block specialist.* Punt rushers who are quick and aggressive who want to block kicks. Aim for the "block point".

- *Team objective.* An all-out effort by blockers who are *intent* on blocking the punt.

FIELD GOAL BLOCK TEAM

- *Objective.* To block the field goal, giving the field goal block team a touchdown or good field position. Always try to advance a blocked kick that hasn't crossed the L.O.S.

- *Block specialist.* Blockers, jumpers, and swimmers. (*Pressure* inside and outside.)

- *Team.* Some players cover for the fake, while the rest are in assigned areas for the block.

- *Extra point blocks.* The true test of the *intensity* of a football team.

KICKOFF RETURN TEAM
(This group can serve as a great field-position weapon, since the kickoff is from the 35-yard line in college and the 40-yard line in high school.)

- *Objective.* To return every kickoff to at least their own 30-yard line.

- *Return specialist.* Returners with fine speed and the desire to "pop" through the wedge. Catch every ball.

- *Team.* Open-field blockers up front, plus a wedge that will block *on the run*. This group of players includes backs to catch short kicks, plus an intelligent "captain of the wedge."

HANDS TEAM

- *Objective.* To recover the ball. Protect the man who recovered it.

- *Specialist.* Quick, aggressive men with good hands.

- *Team.* Recovery men to field the ball. Blockers to protect the recovery men. Two safeties to *handle all kicks* that travel past the front people.

PUNT TEAM

- *Objective.* To gain good field position—less than three yards per return. Force a fair catch. Cause a fumble and recover it. Down the ball inside the 10-yard line.

- *Specialist.* A punter who gets more height than distance and also consistently places the ball on or inside the 10-yard line. A center who makes an accurate snap every time.

- *Team.* Speed is necessary to get to the ballcarrier. Block first. Maintain spacing and never follow the same colored jersey. Break down and then gang tackle. Block-release-cover-tackle.

PUNT FAKES (RUN OR PASS)

- *Objective.* To get the first down or score a touchdown.

- *Specialist.* A personal protector who uses good timing and judgment concerning when to use an automatic run or pass. The most important factor is to get the first down.

- *Team.* Be alert to when and why this weapon is used. All assignments must be carried out for it to be successful. Be alert to *check* to a punt.

FIELD GOAL AND EXTRA POINT TEAM

Keeping in mind that missed field goals outside 20-yard line are returned to the line of scrimmage.

- *Objective.* To score three points (one point-P.A.T.).
- *Specialist.* Three-man partnership:
    - ✓ The kicker to get quick height (to avoid the block) and has consistent accuracy. (1.3 timing)
    - ✓ The holder with sure hands and the ability to quickly place the ball.
    - ✓ The center with rifle accuracy.
- *Team.* No penetration! Take proper splits and steps; see the ball snapped. Cover long field goals.

FIELD GOAL FAKES (RUN OR PASS)

- *Objective.* To get the first down or score a touchdown.
- *Specialist.* A holder with running and passing ability.
- *Team.* Dedicated to carry out pre-assigned responsibilities. No tip-offs.

Remember:	BE SMART!
	HIGH VELOCITY!
	FINISH!

CHAPTER 2

SPECIAL TEAMS ORGANIZATION

Attention to detail in organizing the special teams will provide the means of achieving the "winning edge." There will be some overlapping of the topics in all the chapters of this book, particularly in Chapter 9, that includes a detailed presentation of how the special teams are fitted into the weekly in-season practice schedule. This chapter focuses on the following topics concerning special teams:

- Coaching assignments and responsibilities
- Teaching progressions
- The implementation of the unique rules of the kicking game into the teaching progressions
- Maximizing practice time
- Scouting report and game plan preparation

To implement the organizational structure presented in this chapter and maximize the success of the kicking game, a real commitment is needed to allocate staff meeting time, staff manpower, player meeting time, and practice time. If this allocation becomes a priority, no doubt will exist in the minds of either the coaching staff or the players as to the importance of the kicking game.

COACHING ASSIGNMENTS AND RESPONSIBILITIES

All assistant coaches should have some specific assignments and responsibilities within the six kicking units. It is a bonus when the head coach also becomes directly involved in coaching special teams. His involvement in special teams meetings and practice sends a clear message that the kicking game is important.

The role of the head coach and special teams coordinator are intertwined in several areas, including assistant coaches' assignments, selection of player personnel, game strategy, and game-day decisions regarding the kicking game. Game day substitutions should be handled by the coordinator. Goal charts, grading, scouting report and game plan preparation are also the coordinator's responsibility, with final approval of the head coach.

Each coach should coach as hard and enthusiastically in his kicking assignment as he does when coaching his offensive or defensive position. Every coach and player must realize that when practicing the kicking game, they are preparing to win the "championship."

One of the essential roles in assigning coaching responsibilities is undertaken by the individual or individuals who are responsible for the scout team's organization and execution. Their role is vital to the kicking team's game success. The scout team must be well organized— (i.e., know what to do and how to do it), otherwise, the special teams will suffer. Table 2-1 provides a flow chart that illustrates an example of a suggested chain-of-command regarding special teams.

Table 2-1. Special teams coaching responsibilities.

PERSONNEL	.Head coach and coordinator
GAME DAY DECISIONS	.Head coach and coordinator
SPECIAL TEAMS COORDINATOR	._____
GAME DAY SUBSTITUTIONS	.Coordinator
TIMING (PRACTICE)	.Coaches and kickers
CHARTING (PRACTICE)	.Managers and kickers
PUNTERS	._____
KICKERS	._____
KICK-OFF RETURNERS	._____
PUNT RETURNERS	._____
HOLDERS	._____
SHORT SNAPPER	._____
LONG SNAPPERS	._____
GOAL CHARTS, GRADING, ...	._____
BIG PLAYS, SCOUTING REPORT,	
AND STRATEGY	.Coordinator

*=TEAM LEADER

KICK-OFF COVERAGE AND ONSIDE KICK

ASSIGNMENTS AND ALIGNMENT	.*_____
SPEED TO 30-YARD LINE	._____
1'S & 2'S	._____
3'S & 4'S	._____
5'S	._____
KICKERS	._____
SCOUT TEAM	._____

Table 2-1. Special teams coaching responsibilities. (continued)

KICKOFF RETURN
ASSIGNMENTS AND ALIGNMENT . . . .* _____
RETURNERS . . . . _____
A, B, C, D . . . . _____
FRONT 5 . . . . _____
SCOUT TEAM . . . . _____

PUNT COVERAGE
ASSIGNMENTS AND ALIGNMENT . . . .* _____
MISSILES . . . . _____
T'S AND WING'S . . . . _____
PP, SN, G'S . . . . _____
COVERAGE LANES . . . . _____
SNAPPER . . . . _____
PUNTER TIMING AND STEPS . . . . _____
SCOUT TEAM . . . . _____

PUNT PRESSURE (RETURNS/BLOCKS)
ASSIGNMENTS, ALIGNMENT, AND TECHNIQUES. .* _____
RETURNERS . . . . _____
CORNERS AND #3'S . . . . _____
SCOUT TEAM . . . . _____

FIELD GOAL AND P.A.T. (OFFENSE)
ASSIGNMENTS AND ALIGNMENT . . . .* _____
KICKER AND HOLDER, TIMING . . . . _____
SNAPPER, GUARDS, AND TACKLES . . . . . . _____
L AND R (End) . . . . _____
WINGS . . . . _____

FIELD GOAL AND PAT BLOCK (DEFENSE)
ASSIGNMENTS AND ALIGNMENT . . . .* _____
DL . . . . _____
LB'S . . . . _____
DB'S . . . . _____

TRAITS OF SPECIAL TEAMS PERSONNEL

In general terms, a special teams player should possess the following mental and physical qualities:

- *Intelligence.* Plays smart. Does not commit stupid fouls. Takes the proper angle and makes the correct decisions. These decisions create big plays. Studies this team's scheme so assignments become second nature, which enables him to play with an intelligent, reckless style.

- *Concentration.* Must be mentally in-tune every time he takes the field. Special teams players know when a big play will occur. Special teams players do not get three downs to run three plays. They have only one chance each time to execute properly. Practice concentration is a must. Special teams are limited in the amount of practice repetitions they get during a given week. Every minute must count.

- *"Keeps playing."* Plays until the whistle sounds. A special teams play is never over. After blocking his assigned man, a special teams player should go block someone else! He must never stop playing. All special teams plays take (on the average) 1-2 seconds longer than normal offensive plays. He must stay on his feet and execute the whole play. Special teams players accomplished greatness when they achieve two or three positive things on one special teams play.

- *Plays the full field.* Covers the entire field. Almost every kick requires some type of full-field coverage. Obviously, in a coverage/kick philosophy, where the focus is on reducing the field and eliminating as much open space as possible, the ability to maneuver, cover, block, brake and tackle in an open area is *vital* to a special team's success. A special team player's level of body control and his ability to change directions usually are the difference between making the play and not making the play.

- *Attitude.* Has a great special teams attitude. Plays hard and aggressively. He is always the aggressor and places a major emphasis on big hits. Maintains his mental flexibility. At times, he will be asked to learn more than one position. If injuries occur during the season, a team must put its best combination of players together.

The "specialists" or "skill positions" on special teams—punters, kickers, snappers, holders and returners—must work many extra hours at perfecting their skills. Much of this work will be during unsupervised time, because few college and high school programs have the staff to assign a full-time coach to the kickers. Tables 2-2 to 2-4 present three checklists for kicking specialists that are designed to help them have a productive, unsupervised practice routine.

Table 2-2. An in-season practice schedule for kickers.

SUNDAY

- Warm up & stretch
- Punt during PC period
- Conditioning w/ team

MONDAY

- No practice/no kicking
- Lift
- TCOB – school

TUESDAY

- Pre-practice—warm-up and stretch
- Specialists period – FG'S, punt and KO
- Kick period – PAT/FG'S (TM); punt to returners during PP (10-15)
- KO'S – deep RT & LT from middle, bloop RT and LT
- Conditioning

WEDNESDAY

- Lift
- Pre-practice – warm up and stretch
- Specialists period – FG'S, PUNT, and KO
- Punt drill work prior to kick period – 10" bad snap – 10" mold and drop – 10" line drill
- Kick period – punt cover
- Bike or jog for conditioning

THURSDAY

- Pre-practice – 10 perfect kicks; FG'S and punts
- Kick period – KOC and onside kicks – PC – KOR
- During practice – 10 perfect kicks (pooch, sky and danger) from the -2 yard line
- KO'S – onside RT from LH; drag bunt from middle; squibs from middle

FRIDAY

- Situation/substitution walk-through
- Maybe 6-8 FG'S; punts if the next game is an away game; otherwise, a day of rest and recuperation.

SATURDAY

- *Game day
- Warm up and stretch prior to specialist (10-15 max)
- 10 PAT; FG'S w/snapper and holder
- 12 hit away punts (switch ends after 6 punts); 4 tite punts from the 2 YL
- Three deep KO'S just prior to game

Table 2-3. A practice check list for placekickers and punters.

(Doing it right today, means no regrets tomorrow for placekickers and punters.)

- Assist with ball handling drills as needed (TE'S, receivers, RB'S, etc.).
- Help time and chart when not involved.
- Always stretch and warm-up properly before kicking early.
- Mentally practice when not kicking (visualization and relaxation).
- Do not be a distraction when you have downtime.
- Always be warmed up and ready for "kicking and specialists" periods. This is your chance to compete under game conditions – Be a star!
- Caution – Don't overkick it! It is the quality of your practice that makes you perfect, not the quantity. Kick no more than 50 balls per practice!
- Punters – Do these drills every practice:
  - ✓ Mold and drop mechanics (no steps) – 10 reps
  - ✓ Line drill – Step, drop and leg wing (no kicking) 2 reps sideline to side line – Steps, drop and kick (If cannot kick down the line, use cones or a goal post) 10 kicks.
  - ✓ Bad snap drill – 10 reps
  - ✓ Danger, sky and pooch punts (If not done in specialists period)– 10 total reps
  - ✓ Drills to be completed after kicking period, and other drill work completed.
  - ✓ Plyometric drills – Two foot take-off to double knee touch (ball chest high). (2 sets of 5 reps of each drill)
    - Step to support leg/knee touch (ball chin high)
    - One step to swing leg/knee touch (ball chin high)
    - Full approach to swing foot touch (ball chin high)
  - ✓ Shuffle drill (use cone and tennis ball)
- Place kickers – Do these drills every practice:
  - ✓ Dry runs – 5 reps
  - ✓ No-step drill – 5 reps
  - ✓ One-step drill – 5 reps (use holder or tripod)
  - ✓ Goal post or net drill (for HT) – 5 reps
  - ✓ Down the line drill or sideline FG'S from left and right side – 5, 10, 15, 20 yard line for accuracy 20 kicks total.
  - ✓ Around the world (Use holder or tripod)
- KO'S – once per week. Substitute for punt and PK drill work. Don't do both on same day!
  - ✓ Middle – Deep middle – 2 reps
  - ✓ Deep right –2 reps
  - ✓ Deep left – 2 reps
  - ✓ Squib 2 reps
  - ✓ Left hash – Bloop right 2 reps; Deep left 2 reps (Tuesdays)
  - ✓ Onside RT from LH; drag bunt from middle & LH, squib from middle (Thursdays)
- If your legs are getting tired or sore, substitute some jogging or bike work for kicking after the kick period.

Table 2-4. A skill development checklist for kickers.

PUNTING:

- Hit away (straight)
- Danger (end zone)
- Inside 40-50 (sky and pooch)
- Bad snap
- Angle punting

PAT/FG'S:

- PAT'S
- FG'S (from R, M, L hashmark and all distances)

KO'S:

- Middle – deep middle, deep right, deep left, bloop right, bloop left
- Drag bunt (a surprise KO from the middle)
- Squib – hard (through the front 5 and wedge); soft (to the wedge)
- Left hash – bloop right, deep left
- RT hash – bloop left, deep right
- Left hash – onside right, drag bunt, onside left
- Onside KO situations

The efforts of the specialists should be continually timed and compared to specific, quantitative measures. For example, the snap to the punter should be no more than .08. The time that it takes for a punter to get the ball off (starting from the time the ball leaves the snapper's hands) should be no more than 2.1 seconds. On extra points and field goals, the time from snap to kick should be no more than 1.3 seconds. It takes hours of practice between the snapper, holder and kicker to master this timing.

In selecting starters for each unit, evaluating each player's performance under pressure is most important. Coaches should commit to placing all potential special teams players in game-simulated conditions—either scrimmage or a live action without tackling situations.

"PERFECT 10" DRILL

At the beginning of each season, all new players should be evaluated as to their potential to play special teams. The "Perfect 10" drill is a good exercise for this purpose. New players are graded on a scale of one-to-ten—ten being a perfect score. They are also timed in this drill; thus a score and a time are recorded for each new player. A very close correlation exists between the score and the time. Coaches should have the drill videotaped and shown to all participants.

Furthermore, coaches should also post a ranking of the players' scores and times. Diagram 2-1 illustrates the "Perfect 10."

Without a lot of coaching, this drill enables coaches to evaluate the coverage ability and instincts of their new players and get an idea of which players would best fit their particular coverage teams. The players start at the 50-yard line, on the sideline, and run to the other side of the field along the 50-yard line. Initially, each player weaves through three large pop-up bags that are spread out on the 50-yard line. Coaches evaluate whether a player can run at full speed and weave through the three bags without chopping his feet and slowing down to avoid blockers.

Then, two tall square, lightweight bags are placed on either side of the 50-yard line and held by coaches or managers. As the players approach the two bags, one or both bags will be tossed at shoulder level of the player so that the player running full speed will have to ward off one or both of the bags. This part of the drill gives coaches an indication of the peripheral vision of the coverage man. This trait is very important for a coverage man because it is essential that he is able to see blockers coming at him from either side while running at full speed.

Next, two large square bags are placed on either side of the 50-yard line and held by coaches or managers. The player should run full speed and split the two bags, an action that is similar to the effort involved in splitting a double-team block. Then, as the player comes through the double-team, he then has to run over two bags laying on the ground, that are spaced about three to four yards apart. These bags simulate players that are on the ground. The player has to run full speed and get his feet up and over the players on the ground and still continue his coverage down the field.

Finally, approximately 10 yards past the "step-over" bags and nine yards from the sideline, a cone is positioned where the coverage player is required to come to a "creep." A ballcarrier, standing on the 50-yard line at the sideline, runs either at a 45-degree angle to the tackler's left or right. The coverage player must work "up and in," like a linebacker, and "wrap up" the ballcarrier in a form tackle. If this is a no pads drill, it does not involve "live" tackling, but a "tag-off" situation. To reiterate, this drill is a great tool to evaluate many of the characteristics that are important for a coverage man to be successful.

Many head coaches have philosophical questions regarding the use of offensive and defensive starters on their special teams. The answer to their concerns should be an emphatic, "Yes—use your best players; do not downgrade your special teams by using players of lesser ability." On the other hand, if a team has a backup player who through attitude and effort will play as hard and

"PERFECT 10" DRILL

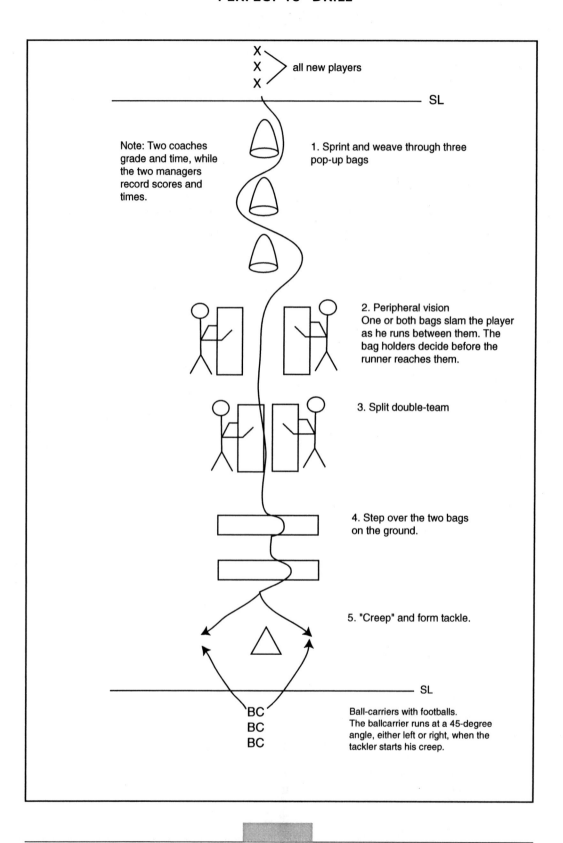

X
X > all new players
X

SL

Note: Two coaches grade and time, while the two managers record scores and times.

1. Sprint and weave through three pop-up bags

2. Peripheral vision
One or both bags slam the player as he runs between them. The bag holders decide before the runner reaches them.

3. Split double-team

4. Step over the two bags on the ground.

5. "Creep" and form tackle.

SL

BC
BC
BC

Ball-carriers with footballs. The ballcarrier runs at a 45-degree angle, either left or right, when the tackler starts his creep.

fast and as effectively as a starter, then he should be a special teams starter. The key point to remember is that a coach should not sacrifice skill, speed and ability in the kicking game. Furthermore he should sell the starters on the concept that if they need a rest, they will not play a series on offense or defense. By the same token, they will not get a rest break for a special teams play. Another concept to sell starters is that if they are not starting on at least two kicking units, "there is a flaw in your armor."

Organizing and Implementing Teaching Progressions

One of the mistakes many coaching staffs make is to approach special teams differently than they do the coaching/teaching of their offensive and defensive schemes. Most coaches believe in the part-whole method of teaching—first techniques and fundamentals—then the player's assignments—then the schemes or plays.

As an example, a wide receiver coach may teach a progression that includes: wide receivers releases and route stems, the footwork involved in a break, and catching fundamentals. Then, he will teach the routes and the patterns. This example can be used with every position on the offense and the defense. But, many coaches do not do that with the kicking game. Instead, they will line up eleven players, kick the ball, and expect those players to be able to execute the required fundamentals and techniques without ever *teaching* them the basic aspects involved. Players might know the scheme, and they may know what they are trying to do, but they do not know how to do it. That is a critical mistake. The teaching process for special teams should include the following four phases in order to be successful:

- Meetings
- Practice
- Walk-throughs
- Follow-up

To properly plan teaching progressions for the season, a "Special Teams Insertion Calendar" should be developed. Table 2-5 illustrates an example of a pre-season practice calendar that includes all special teams work leading up to the first game. It has a daily breakdown of meetings, walk-throughs, and practices for every phase of the kicking game. This calendar includes the "what and when" so that coaches and players can prepare themselves in advance for the appropriate meetings and practice sessions. The calendar also has a section where the total number of meetings, practices, and walk-throughs for each kicking team is shown. This feature allows the coach to easily see the amount of time scheduled for each unit. Of course, the most time should be spent on the kicking team that is the most difficult to master, (i.e., punt cover).

Table 2.5 Sample pre-season special teams insertion calendar.

SUNDAY	MONDAY	TUESDAY	WEDNESDAY	THURSDAY	FRIDAY	SATURDAY
			2	3 Newcomers report	4 Newcomers Practice #1 & #2 Perfect 10 Drill	5 Newcomers Practice #3 & 4
6	7 PM TEAM REPORTS	8 -Conditioning test -Orientation -Meetings	9 AM (NP) -PC walk through -PC PM (NP) -PC -PC meeting	10 AM(NP) -PC Walk thru -PC PM (NP) -Specialists -PC -PC meetiong	11 AM (NP) -PC Walk thru -PC PM (NP) -Specialists -PC -FG & FGB meeting	12 AM(pads) -FG & FGB walk thru -FG & FGB PM (pads) -specialists -PC -PC Meeting
13 AM(pads) -PC walk thru -PC PM (shells) -specialists -PP hold-up drills -1/2 game conditioning - PP meeting	14 NO PRACTICE DAY & NO MEETINGS	15 AM(pads) -PP walk thru -PP block drills PM (pads) -specialists -PP. maroon, black & brown -PP meeting	16 AM(pads) -PP walk thru -PP rip & liz (80 & 60) PM (pads) -specialists & PC walk thru -PC scrimmage -FG/FGB during scrim -no meetings (grade tape)	17 AM(NP) -scrimmage tape -KOR walk thru -KOR drills -KOC invite letter PM (pads) -specialists -KOR (slam rt) -KOC meeting	18 AM(pads) -KOC walk thru -KOC drills PM (NP) -Specialists -KOC-time ups & covers vs. return's R&L -PC meeting 1. sat scrim 2. wed pc tape	19 AM Scrimmage -PC scrimmage -FG VS FGB during scrimmage Lunch awards
20 -KOR (slam left) 1/2 game conditioning	21 NO PRACTICE DAY & CLASSES BEGIN	22 -PC meeting(sat PC scrimmage tape) -specialists -PC 1. 1/2 line 2. 2 on 2 drill	23 -PP meeting -specialists -Review maroon black, brown	24 -dress rehearsal scrimmage *scout team meet to organize for scrimmage	25 (NP) -PC meeting (scrim tape) -KOC vs. opponent returns	26 -hands -devil sharks -safe" punt return
27 No practice	28 Pads(night) -PP meeting (game plan) -specialists 1. FG vs. FGB 2. PP	29 Pads -KOR meeting -PC meeting -specialists -PC -KOR after practice	30 (NP) -KOC meeting -PP meeting -PC -KOC & devil sharks -KOR "perfect wednesday"	31 -KOR meeting -PC meeting -sub. script practice	1 SEPTEMBER FIRST GAME	2

Another helpful organizational tool is the in-season meeting and practice schedule. This schedule includes the daily special teams meetings, walk-throughs and practice during game week. This schedule is discussed in detail in Chapter 9 because of its implications regarding game-plan preparation.

With these two organizational tools, the coach can prioritize what is most important, and the aspects that need the most time. Collectively, they provide coaches with an invaluable system of "checks and balances" in planning. It also allows the coaches and players to get into a routine that becomes familiar to them.

In most situations, the time allocated for special teams meetings is limited. Therefore, it is important to be well organized. A special teams bulletin board can be very helpful in getting pertinent and timely information to the team. Among the items that should be posted daily are:

- A motivational quote or phrase to get their attention.
- A meetings and practice schedule to inform them of the "what-where-when."
- An updated special teams depth chart ("the who").
- The pre-practice "specialists period" depth chart.
- Scout team depth chart for that day.

For all special teams meetings, materials should be prepared in advance, and set out and ready to go because there is no time to waste. Every meeting should always start on time to get the material covered, and allow the players to get to their next meeting on time. The presentation should be clear and pre-cise, and should move quickly to cover all of the necessary information. It is imperative, the coach should exude enthusiasm and excitement for what he is doing.

Another effective technique in gaining the respect and attention of the play-ers during these meetings is to organize the room so that the starters sit in the front row by position. The backup players sit behind the starters. This seating arrangement also gives the coach a quick visual check to see if all personnel are "present and accounted for." In order to ensure that each meeting is as pro-ductive as possible, the coach should emphasize the players apply the SLANT principle while in these meetings: sit up; lean forward; act interested; nod your head; track the coach.

"The Specialists Period Depth Chart" is shown in Table 2-6. This special teams tool alerts the kickers and snappers as to when to be warmed up and ready to kick. If specialists will be rotated from one skill to another on a daily basis, this depth chart will tell them what to do that particular day. Furthermore, it avoids having coaches waste time informing and moving players around the field during this period. It should also be noted that other groups of players could be working on some phase of the kicking game during this period. For example, the offensive linemen and tight ends could walk-through field-goal protection and/or fakes. Still another example would be to have the defense walk-through field-goal block assignments.

Table 2-6. Daily specialists period depth chart

Punt returners:		KO returners:	
_____		_____	
_____		_____	
_____		_____	
_____		_____	
Punters:		Kickoff kickers (rotate kickers):	
_____		_____	
_____		_____	
_____		_____	
_____		_____	
Long snappers:	Short snappers:	Kickers:	Holders:
_____	_____	_____	_____
_____	_____	_____	_____
_____	_____	_____	_____
_____	_____	_____	_____

The organization of the scout team is another factor that needs a lot of attention in order to have productive kicking practices. A good starting place is to post the scout team personnel for that day—the players on the scout team and what position they will play. For example, the coach could diagram a punt team with a scout punt-defense team. Then, put the names of the scout team on the diagram by the position they are going to be role-playing during the kicking period. As the season progresses, it is best to stay with the same personnel on the scout teams and be as consistent as possible so that the scout team players do not have to learn multiple techniques and assignments. During the season, in particular, the scout team consists primarily of red-shirt freshmen or walk-on players who are backups and not projected to be on the travel squad.

Good effort and enthusiasm are must-have qualities from the scout-team group in order to properly prepare the kicking units. Occasionally, the scout team coach should meet with the players assigned to the special scout team units for organizational purposes. This step will help maximize the time available during practices because the scout team will know what to do.

Even though scout teams play an important role in preparing the kicking units, coaches should make every effort to practice "good-versus-good." This would include individual, segment and team situations. For example, the coach could match-up the punt cover unit with the punt return/block unit to provide "good-versus-good" practice repetitions.

The scout team should also be used in walk-throughs. In addition, the scout team coach should have all the opponent schemes on cards. This procedure is the same as having the scout offense and scout defense working off of cards so that they know what they're supposed to be doing. For example, the opponent's one or two favorite kick-off returns should be on cards with the names of the scout team on the card by position. As a result, the scout players will know where to line-up and what to do. Wasted time and missed assignments can be minimized by using cards.

Walk-through situations are often very effective in the teaching progression. Generally, walk-throughs are conducted prior to practice. Irregardless, they should be done in an organized manner. Walk-throughs can emphasize any number of factors, including a combination of schemes, assignments, or drill organization. Furthermore, scout team personnel should be used so that they also learn what is required of them during the kicking period later in practice.

The third phase in the teaching progression is practice. It is important to first practice individual skills. There are many fundamentals and techniques that are essential in the kicking game that are not required (and thus, not taught) in offensive and defensive practices. It should be noted that some carryover exists between the kicking game and other facets of play, particularly with defensive personnel in regard to coverage principles, and tackling fundamentals. As a point of fact, however, most of the fundamentals and techniques involved in the kicking game are not taught in other aspects of the game.

It is important to break the kicking game down into individual skills and teach those first and then work into segment or group work against the scout team, or "good-versus-good." Then, and only then, after individual and segment drills, should team situations be practiced. Special teams need to be tested. The most effective way to evaluate special teams in a practice situation is by scrimmaging or engaging in live situations without tackling.

The fourth phase in teaching progressions is follow-up. This step involves a review of practice and game video with those coaches who are responsible for that phase of the kicking game, and then review with the players. The players need to see and evaluate the practice and game video in order to improve. They improve not only by visualizing the correct way to perform a skill, but also by visualizing their assignment or technique errors to make corrections in a visual sense.

UNDERSTANDING THE RULES

In many instances, the rules of the kicking game are very different than those on offense or defense. In these instances, they are unique and are often not well understood by the players. The rules involving the kicking game need to be covered in a variety of different ways. A good starting point is to acquire an illustrated rules book—a rules book with cartoon-type characters that interprets and explains along with the illustrations. The coach can then make transparencies of the illustrated rules, particularly the unique and not well-understood rules and use that transparency to illustrate the rule during a meeting. This step will only take a few seconds, and hopefully, it will make a lasting impression.

Coaches also need to address rule applications and infractions as they occur on the practice field. If a rule infraction occurs during practice, it is a good idea to briefly stop the drill work and explain the rule infraction and application as it occurs, rather than waiting for another time.

MAXIMIZING PRACTICE TIME

Because meeting and practice time for special teams is usually limited, coaches should be extremely well organized and efficient in order to maximize the time that is available. In reality there will never be enough practice time for special teams. Therefore, not only be super organized, but be creative in the use of the allocated time. This also involves pre-practice, during practice and post-practice time slots.

When an individual is coaching the kicking game, it is extremely important to be sensitive about how he practices the players, particularly if he inserts kicking at the beginning or middle of practice. The players must have the energy and the enthusiasm to complete an approximately two-hour practice. Thus, it is not necessary to have the special teams players do a lot of long distance running. As a rule, most special teams' plays involve 40 or more yards, with the exception of PAT's and field goals. However, a coach does not need to run his players on 40-50 yard sprints in order to achieve his practice objectives. This factor should be taken into consideration when developing teaching progressions and drills that are used with the special teams. Also, by constricting the practice field, a greater number of repetitions can be accomplished in a shorter time period.

Previously, the point was made that insertion schedules for the in-season, as well as pre-season, need to be employed to make sure that all aspects of special teams are covered and practiced. Tables 2-7 to 2-8 present two practice checklists that can be used to make sure that all necessary fundamentals, techniques, assignments, and game situations will be practiced and rehearsed prior to playing in a game. In Table 2-7, for example, the "Special Teams Practice Checklist" provides a list of 26 different team situations, an overview of individual specialties involved in special teams play, and a group or segment checklist for the six kicking units.

Table 2-7. Special teams practice checklist.

SPECIAL SITUATIONS – TEAM
• Punting from the hashmarks
• Punting from the end zone
• Punting from the 45-50 yard line
• Punting from bad-snap situations
• Covering the fair catch
• Reaction to a blocked kick (punt, FG, & PAT)
• Reaction to a partially blocked kick
• Receiving punts deep in own territory
• Rushing punts when opponent is backed up to his goal line
• Prevent on punt defense
• Reacting to fake punts
• Onside kickoff
• Onside kickoff return (hands team)
• Surprise onside kickoff defense
• Squib kickoffs
• Returning squib and short kickoffs
• Bad snap on PAT and field goal attempts (fire)
• Field goal prevent
• Defensing fake field goals
• "Scramble" field goal (no time-outs)
• Unbalanced line field goals
• Defensing unbalanced-line field goals
• Defensing swinging-gate field goals
• Taking an intentional safety
• Kickoff after a safety
• Receiving a kickoff after a safety

Table 2-7. Special teams practice checklist (continued).

SPECIAL SITUATIONS — INDIVIDUAL SPECIALTIES
- Punting—hash mark:
  - ✓ End zone (danger)
  - ✓ Inside 45-50 (sky)
  - ✓ Bad snap
  - ✓ Against wind
  - ✓ Scramble and punt
  - ✓ Quick kick
- Center snap:
  - ✓ Punt
  - ✓ PAT and field goal
- Placekicking (Kickoff):
  - ✓ Deep
  - ✓ Squib
  - ✓ Right hash, deep
  - ✓ Middle, onside left & right, drag bunt
  - ✓ Right hash, onside left
  - ✓ Left hash, deep
  - ✓ Left hash, onside right
- Receiving punts:
  - ✓ Safety communications (Peter)
  - ✓ Fair catch
  - ✓ 10-yard line
  - ✓ Fielding grounders
- Receiving kickoffs:
  - ✓ Safety communications
  - ✓ Squib & bloop kickoff
  - ✓ Onside kickoff
- Blocking kicks:
  - ✓ Punts
  - ✓ Place kicks
- Placekick holder:
  - ✓ Normal
  - ✓ Bad snap

GROUP OR TEAM SEGMENTS
- Punting:
  - ✓ Splits and alignment
  - ✓ Zone & man blocking (short drill)
  - ✓ Coverage (long drill)
    - Release from the LOS
    - Lanes (spread the net)
    - Close the gate
    - Containment
    - Pursuit angles
    - Middle and hash
  - ✓ tackling angles
- Punt defense:
  - ✓ Alignment
  - ✓ Stem procedure
  - ✓ Blocking upfield
  - ✓ Hold-up techniques
  - ✓ Block techniques
  - ✓ Release to set the wall

Table 2-7. Special teams practice checklist (continued).

- ✓ Punt block alignment and angles
- ✓ Setting up wall
  - middle
  - hash
- Kickoff:
  - ✓ Coverage
    - Avoiding frontline blocks
    - fill and force angles
    - defeating single and double-team blocks
    - pursuit angles
  - ✓ tackling angles
  - ✓ recover onside KO's
- Kickoff Returns:
  - ✓ Front five:
    - cross blocking
    - recovering surprise onside kickoff
    - setting up a wall from the middle, right and left hashmarks
    - wedge blocking
    - onside kickoffs
  - ✓ Safety
    - communications
    - fielding squibs and bloops
    - wedge relationship to safeties
    - setting the wedge
- PAT and field goal:
  - ✓ Alignment
  - ✓ Protection techniques:
    - coverage
    - release from the LOS
    - lanes (spread the net)
    - close the gate
    - containment
    - pursuit angles
    - middle snf hash
  - ✓ tackling angles
- PAT & field goal defense:
  - ✓ Alignment
  - ✓ Block alignment and angles
  - ✓ Fakes
  - ✓ Swinging gate

The "Kicking Game Daily Implementation Checklist" presented in Table 2-8 is another tool that can be used to make sure that all special teams meetings, practice, and situations are covered during the week of practice.

Table 2-8. Kicking game — daily implementation checklist.

PUNT TEAM:
- Meeting
- Hit and releases
- Coverage lanes
- Zone protection
- "Sky" punt
- "Danger" punt
- Stacks
- Basic protection
- Fakes

KICK-OFF RETURN:
- Meeting
- Right return
- Convert left
- KOR left and convert
- Free kick return
- Short and "squib" kicks
- Hands team
- Middle or wide field return

P.A.T. FIELD GOAL:
- Meeting
- Right and left
- P.A.T.
- No-huddle field goal
- Fakes
- "FIRE" call

PUNT RETURN:
- Meeting
- Right return
- Left return
- Middle return
- Prevent return
- Blocks
- Receive sky punt
- Stop fakes

KICKOFF COVER:
- Meeting
- Right or left
- Release and cover Lanes
- Onside kick
- Free kick (punter)
- Surprise or bloop kick

FIELD GOAL BLOCK:
- Meeting
- Right or left
- Middle swim pinch
- 11-man block
- Defend swinging gate
- No huddle field goal
- Stop fakes

In summary, practice periods should include: 1) a specialist period, either pre- or post-practice where kickers, snappers, holders, returners, and any other specialists can develop their individual skills; 2) kicking periods that develop team concepts through the part-whole method of teaching, just like a coach teaches his offense and defense; 3) testing of the kicking game through live but no tackling, or scrimmage situations; and 4) follow-up meetings to critique practice video.

SCOUTING AND GAME PLAN PREPARATION

The next phase of the organization of special teams is scouting and game planning. This chapter only presents a general approach to this issue because a separate and more detailed scouting and game-plan presentation appears in Chapter 9. Chapter 9 addresses several factors, including: how a game plan and scouting report are put together; how a game plan is formulated from the scouting report; scouting report forms and diagrams; and the development of training tapes of an opponent. In this chapter, however, the point to keep in mind is that the game plan needs to be based on a thorough and comprehensive study and charting of an opponent's kicking game.

As part of scouting and game plan preparation, it is appropriate to talk about one of the most critical areas in game management — the substitution of special teams personnel to insure that the right players are on the field at the "right" time. It is critical not to come up with too few players, or have too many players on the field in kicking-game situations. Unfortunately, this occurs too often. The penalties and time-outs that occur are not only an embarrassment to everyone involved, but also hurtful to the team.

Doing special teams substitution properly can happen, but not without prior preparation. During the week of practice, a need exists to have not only starters, but also designated backups, so that if a starter is injured or unable to participate, a substitute will be prepared and ready to go on the field. It is also the responsibility of the backup players on the sidelines to be alert. If they see a player is hurt, they should identify that player and bring it to the special teams coaches' attention. The medical staff should also make it clear to the coach as to whether that player is unable to participate. Furthermore, they should also communicate to the special teams coach at a later date if that player becomes cleared and ready to go back on the field, so the change can be made with his backup if it is deemed necessary to do so.

Two forms and charts that can be very helpful in keeping track of special teams personnel are illustrated in Tables 2-9 and 2-10. The first is a "Special Teams Depth Chart" (Table 2-9) that lists both starters and backup players.

Table 2-9. Special teams depth chart A

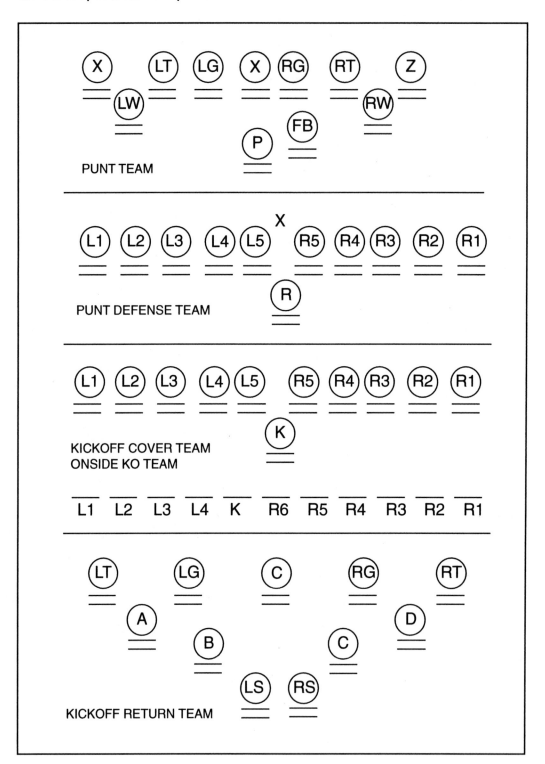

Table 2-9. Special teams depth chart B

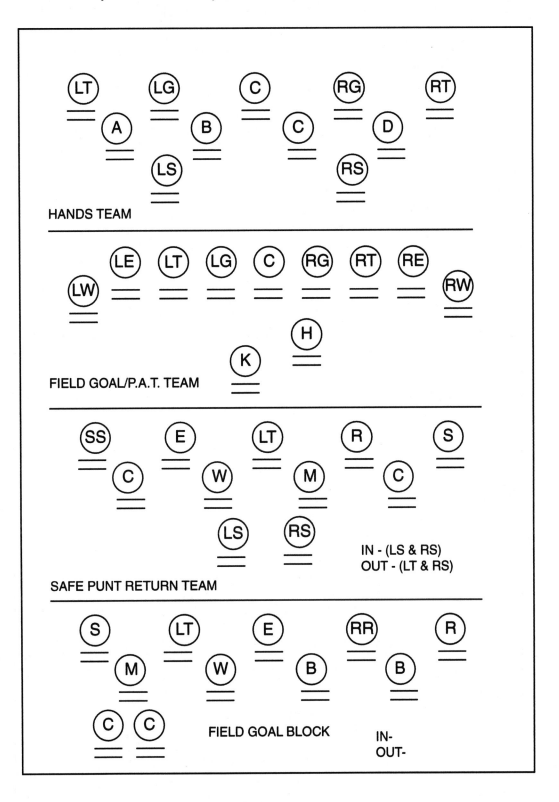

HANDS TEAM

FIELD GOAL/P.A.T. TEAM

IN - (LS & RS)
OUT - (LT & RS)

SAFE PUNT RETURN TEAM

FIELD GOAL BLOCK

IN-
OUT-

Another invaluable tool is called "The Special Teams Participation List" (Table 2-10). This form lists all offensive and defensive players by position and then, after their name, the special teams units they are on, and whether they are a starter (designated by # 1), or a backup (designated by # 2). For example, John Smith is a corner and after his name there would be a 1PC. That designation would indicate that he is a starter on the punt cover unit. Two other examples are 1PR (one punt return) and 1KOC (one kickoff cover). As a result, if that player, John Smith, got hurt, the coach would go to the participation list and quickly see that he is a starter on three units. Then, he would look at the depth chart and find his backup, or backups, for those units. The coach would then communicate to the backup that he is now the starter. If situations occur where several key special teams players are hurt and unable to play, this type of information is necessary to make sure that backups are ready and on the field at the appropriate time.

Table 2-10. The special teams participation list.

SPECIAL TEAMS PARTICIPATION LIST		
Defensive Backs	Position	Special Teams
John Smith	CB	1 PC; 1 PR; 1 KOC
Running Backs		
Bill Jones	FB	1 PC; 1 KOR

Some teams use what is commonly referred to as the "hot box" or the "launch pad" procedure—an area designated along the sideline where the special teams players report on the third down. For example, the punt team reports to the box area on third down, and the coach responsible for that unit makes sure that he has the proper personnel ready to go into the game. Some starters on that unit may already be on the field, so the coach should use his "depth chart" and "participation list" to check who those players are.

Another criteria for "perfect" substitution is to be aware of certain situations in the game where the potential exists for more than one unit being substituted. One example might be a long field-goal situation where a potential exists for three different events occurring. The first option would be to keep the offense on the field to run a fourth-down play. The second option would be to substitute the field goal unit and attempt a field goal. The third option would be to substitute the punt team on fourth down and sky or pooch punt (i.e., an attempt to down the kick inside the 10-yard line). All these units have to be alert. They cannot assume anything, and they should be ready to go onto the field based on what the fourth-down call is.

Conversely, if a team's opponent is in plus territory (i.e., across the 50-yard line) and in a situation where either a field goal or a punt is possible, coaches must be alert to their substitution possibilities so that the right call can be made. Furthermore, if they conclude that it may be appropriate to put their punt team on the field, a decision must be made to either send the punt return unit onto the field, or keep the defense on the field in what is commonly referred to as a "safe" return personnel group. Even with the "safe" return called, the returner would have to be substituted. Thus, communication needs to be perfect in these situations. Table 2-11 presents a "punt/field goal situations" chart that illustrates the primary decision-making areas on the field concerning these types of situations.

Table 2-11. Punt/field goal situations chart.

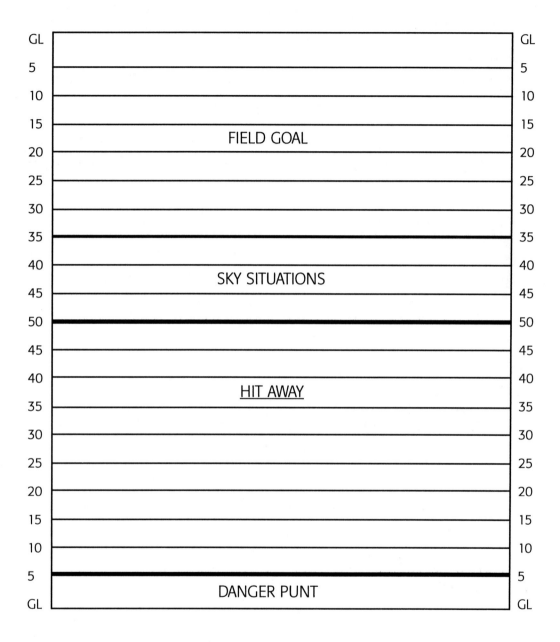

GL		GL
5		5
10		10
15	FIELD GOAL	15
20		20
25		25
30		30
35		35
40	SKY SITUATIONS	40
45		45
50		50
45		45
40	HIT AWAY	40
35		35
30		30
25		25
20		20
15		15
10		10
5	DANGER PUNT	5
GL		GL

CHAPTER 3

GRADING AND AWARDS

Most of the business world relies heavily on "quality control" to make and sell a money-making product. Football coaches involved with special teams should do the same to give their squad the "winning edge."

Many ways exist to grade player performance, to assess goals accomplished, and to award players for outstanding performance. The importance lies in the fact that special teams player's performance is evaluated, goals are assessed as to whether they are accomplished or not, and players are recognized for outstanding performance. It is just as important for these processes to occur with the special teams as it is with the offensive and defensive units. If the time and effort are not given to these processes, a message is sent to the entire team that special teams is not as important as the offense and defense. Furthermore, in most situations, since special teams receive little media attention, it is even more important to make the effort internally—within the program—to stress the special teams' accomplishments.

This chapter addresses three ways to efficiently accomplish "quality control" regarding special teams:

- Grading of individual player performance
- Goals assessment
- Player recognition and awards

GRADING INDIVIDUAL PLAYER PERFORMANCE

As a rule, because colleges have more resources and manpower than most high school situations, some adjustments typically may have to be made to the process for grading individual performance on special teams, depending on the program's resources. Regardless of the adjustment, grading is highly beneficial in evaluating an individual's performance on the kicking units. Grading is beneficial because it provides a more objective means of determining overall performance, not only for single games, but also for all games as the season progresses. Grading also helps make personnel decisions somewhat easier by providing an objective means of determining which players are either playing well or poorly. Obviously, the player who is consistently receiving poor grades should be replaced.

The six "grading summary" forms illustrated in Tables 3-1 to 3-6 can be altered to better suit each program's available grading resources. The names of the starters on each of the six kicking units can be inserted prior to the grading process. Substitutes that actually get into the game can be listed below the starters, as the coaches are grading. Then, as each play is evaluated, the information columns at the top of the form are completed before grading the players on that play. This information is very important because it will provide a summary of statistics that is needed to complete the "goal sheets" discussed later in this chapter. The following grade key—each number is color-coded as indicated—can be used for each kicking play:

- 3 (Green) = Big play
- 2 (Black) = Good effort and execution
- 1 (Blue) = Poor effort or execution
- 0 (Red) = Critical error

It may be easier for the grading coach to write in black ink. He can then go back and use colored felt pens to fill-in those boxes with 3's, 1's, or 0's. This system of grading provides a high degree of objectivity to the grading process. It is also important to insert comments in the "comments" column, particularly if inserting a grade other than a 2 (black). This procedure provides a handy reference for addressing any questions a player may have regarding a grade received.

Upon completing the grading process, the "grade summary" forms should be posted where all players can see them. This step can be accomplished by having a "grade board" that allows the posting of each 8 1/2 x 11 grading summary. It can be as graphic and fancy as resources allow. An example of what this board might look like is illustrated in Table 3-7.

As was stated in Chapter I, approximately 90-100 big plays in the kicking game occur over the course of a season. Thus, it is important for a team to assess how many big plays are made for and against it. The "Special Teams Big Plays" chart illustrated in Table 3-8 can be used both as a team grading tool and as a way of recognizing individual big plays. Because big plays are recorded on the "grading summary" forms, it is an easy process to transpose the big plays in a game onto this chart. It is also a good idea to have a "board" developed so that big plays can be added on a game-by-game basis as the season progresses.

Table 3-1. A sample kickoff return grading summary form.

Play	Time	Kick To	Return	Returner	Return Yds	Start	Comments	POS	Names	| 1	2	3	4	5	6	7	8	9	10 |	Avg	Big Play
1	1:44 / 1st	14	RT	Williams	30	A44		LT	Dennard	2	2	2	1							1.75	
2	4:08 / 2nd	18	"	"	13	A21	avg yds 15 th penalty from 20 holding +43	LG	Johnson	1	2	2	1							1.5	
3	15:00 / 2nd	19	Crafer	"	–	A19		C	Rance	1	1	2	1							1.25	1
4	8:57 / 3rd	17	Ctr	Teplin	11	A23		RG	O'Neal	3	2	2	2							2.25	1
								RT	Fulton	3	2	2	1							2	1
								A	Maddox	2	2	2	2							2	1
					18.0	28.0		B	Brooks	2	2	2	2							2	1
					avg Return	avg Start		C	Fox	3	1	1	2							1.75	1
								D	Waddell	3	0	1	2							1.5	1
								LS	Teplin	2	2	2	2							2	
								RS	R. Williams	3	2	1	1							1.75	1

GAME:

Kick-Off Return

Table 3-2. A sample kickoff coverage grading summary form.

GAME:

Play	Hash	Kick To	Return Yds	Start	Tackled By	Comments	POS	Names	1	2	3	4	5	6	7	8	9	10	Avg	Big Play
1	13:00 1st	EZ	TB	W20		Touchback	L1	Taplin	2	2	2	1							1.8	
2	5:54 1st	EZ	TB	W20		"	L2	Wilson	2	2	2	1							1.8	
3	3:12 1st	EZ	TB	W20		"	L3	Rance	2	2	2	3							2.4	2
4	2:08 2nd	20	22	W42	Demeterio T / Aguirre T	KO from 20yl other 5 team	L4	Hogue	2	2	2	1							1.8	
5	1:04 2nd	1	36	W27	Demeterio T / Rance AT	Holding penalty	L5	Aguirre	2	2	2	3	2						2.2	1
							K	Barth	3	3	2	2	2						2.4	2
							RS	Fulton	2	2	2	2	2						2	
		29		21:7 on KO from 35 yl			R4	Ware	2	1	1	1	1						1.2	
		Avg. Return					R3	Falkner	2	2	3	2							2.2	1
							R2	Koontz	2	2	2	1							1.8	
					1st to 30 YL		R1	Demeterio	2	2	2	3	3						2.4	2
					1 Aguirre															
					2 Wilson															
					3 Wilson / Koontz															
					4 Koontz															
					5 Wilson															

Grade Key: 3(green) = Big play; 2(black) = Good effort & execution;
1(blue) = Poor effort or execution; O(red) = Critical error

Table 3-3. A sample field goal block grading summary form.

Play	Hash	LOS	Spot	Cal	Success	PGS	Comments	Names	1	2	3	4	5	6	7	8	9	10	Avg	Big Play
		20	26	S.R.	Good			Wellin	2	2	2								2	
		Xpoint		D.P.	Good			Pinkard	2	2	2								2	
		25	31	S.R.	No Good			Yancy	2	2	2								2	
								Glass	2	2	2								2	
								Fields	2	2									2	
								Bates	2	2	2								2	
								Anderson	2	2	2								2	
								Blake	2	2	2								2	
								K.Williams	1	2	1								1.3	
								A.Williams	2	2	2								2	
								Clay	2	2	2								2	

Table 3-4. A sample field goal – PAT grading summary form.

Play	Hash	LOS	Spot	Success	Penetration	Comments	POS	Names	Field Goal - PAT 1	2	3	4	5	6	7	8	9	10	Avg	Big Play
1	M	34	52	NG		Wide RT	LW	Trejo	2	2	2	2	0	0	3				1.57	1
2			PAT	G			L	Maddox	2	2	2	2	0	0	3				1.57	1
3			PAT	G			LT	Leyva	2	2	2	2	2	2	3				2.1	1
4			PAT	Muffed snap		First failed / Complete to	LG	Crawford	2	2	2	2	2	2	3				2.1	1
5	LM	19	36	NG			SN	Breckinridge	2	2	2	1	2	1	3				1.85	1
6	M	18		Muffed snap recd by Barth			RG	Hogue	2	2	2	2	2	2	2				2.1	1
7	M	24	41	G			R	Jones	2	2	2	2	2	2	3				2.1	1
							R	Moore	2	2	2	2	2	2	3				2.1	1
					PATs 2-3		RW	Heep	2	1	2	2	2	2	3				2	1
					FG's 1-3		H	Goodman	2	2	2	0	2	1	3				1.7	1
							K	Barth	0	2	2	0	3	3					1.7	2

Table 3-5. A sample punt coverage grading summary form.

GAME:										Tackled		Punt Coverage													Big
Play	Hash	LOS	Situation	Call	Front	Punt Yds	Return	Net	Start	By	Comments	POS	Names	1	2	3	4	5	6	7	8	9	10	Avg	Play
1		W49	0:16 1st	Blue	40 SAFE	49	TB	49	W20		Touchback	X	Denesto	1	2	2		3	2	2				2	1
2		A23	9:27 2nd	Lawn	OVLD LT	39	0	39	W39		Downed	Z	Rance	1	2	2		2	2	2				1.83	
3a		A39	6:08 2nd	Lawn	OVLD LT	29	0				Delay Penalty/offsides	LW	Palma	2	2	2		2	2	2				2	
3		A44	6:03 2nd	"	OVLD LT	26	0	26	30W		Out of Bounds	LT	Heap	2	2	2		2	2	2				2	
4		A15	2:03 2nd	"	"						Snap over punter's head for safety	LG	Trejo	2	2	2		2	2	2				2	
5		W48	11:32 3rd	"	"	37	5	32	W16	Denesto		SN	Buckenridge	1	1	2	0	1	2	2				1.2	
6		W36	5:04 3rd	Blue	SAFE 40	36	TB	36	W20		Touchback	RG	Fox	2	2	2		2	2	2				2	
7		W40	11:31 4th	Red	"	30	08	30	W10		Out of Bounds	RT	Hogue	2	2	2		2	2	2				2	
												RW	A-Williams	2	2	2		2	2	2				2	
						36.0		35.9				FB	Koontz	2	2	2		2	2	2				2	
						avg.		Net				P	Murphy	2	2	1		2	1	3				1.83	1

Table 3-6. A sample punt return grading summary form.

GAME: _____

Play	Hash	LOS	Call	Punt Yds	Return Yds	Start	Net	Returner	Comments	POS	Names	1	2	3	4	5	6	7	8	9	10	Avg	Big Play
1	5:32 1st	W20	65 Ret	36	47	W17	-11	Taplin		LC	Palmer	3	1	2	1							1.75	1
2	12:38 2nd	A45	Safe	32	OB	A13	32	"	Out of Bounds #50 Pembry	RC	Ramer	3	3	3	2							2.25	2
3	3:52 2nd	W43	63 L2	44	Downed	A13	44	"	Downed	L1	O'Neal	2	2	3	2							2.25	1
4	1:49 2nd	W35	80 L2	0		W35	0	Falkner	Blocked by Anuesto Recd Falkner	L2	Falkner	3	2	5	2							2.5	2
5	9:04 3rd	W18	Return	31	Downed	W49	31	Taplin	Downed	L5	Wilson	3	2	3	2							2.5	2
										L4	Demerts	3	2	3	2							2.5	2
				28.6	47.0		19.4			R4	Hogue	3	1	3	2							2.35	2
				Avg.	Avg.		Net			R3	Koontz	3	2	3	2							2.5	2
					Return					R2	Brooks	3	2	3	2							2.5	2
										R1	K.Williams	3	2	5	2							2.5	2
										R	Taplin	3	2	2	2	2						2.2	1

Table 3-7. A sample special teams game grades board.

Punt Coverage

Names	1	2	3	4	5	6	7	8	9	10	Avg	Big Play

Kick Off Coverage

Names	1	2	3	4	5	6	7	8	9	10	Avg	Big Play

Field Goal - PAT

Names	1	2	3	4	5	6	7	8	9	10	Avg	Big Play

Punt Return

Names	1	2	3	4	5	6	7	8	9	10	Avg	Big Play

Kick Off Return

Names	1	2	3	4	5	6	7	8	9	10	Avg	Big Play

Field Goal Block

Names	1	2	3	4	5	6	7	8	9	10	Avg	Big Play

Grade key: 3 = big play; 2 = good effort or execution; 1 = poor effort or execution; 0 = critical error

Table 3-8. A sample "special teams big plays chart.

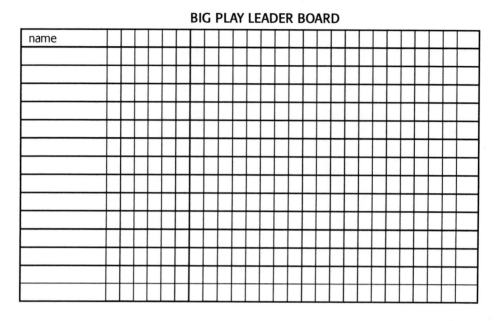

BIG PLAY LEADER BOARD

name																																	

- Punt coverage tackle for return of 3-or-less yards
- Kickoff coverage tackle inside the 20-yard line.
- Cause or recover a fumble.
- Kick or recover an onside kickoff (ours or opponent).
- Punt or down a punt inside the 10-yard line.
- Block a punt, PAT, or FG.
- Successful fake or fire.
- Stop a fourth-down fake.
- Kick return for TD or a 3-point PAT.
- Kickoff return to 40 plus yardline.
- 25-yard punt return.
- Key block on a TD return, a 40-yard KOR, or a 25-yard punt return.

GOALS ASSESSMENT

The second aspect of quality control is the assessment of whether the special teams are accomplishing the specified kicking-game goals. In this regard, it is important to keep in mind that the goals of special teams should be attainable, but not too easy. In other words, they should be realistic. The players should also be involved in establishing these goals. As a rule, if they are a part of the process of setting these goals, they will have more of a vested interested in accomplishing the goals. It is recommended that a goal "board" be developed so that goals can be posted on a game-by-game basis for the entire season, including any non-regularly scheduled contests, such as bowl games, play-off games, etc.

The level of complexity of special teams goals is simply a subjective matter of choice by the coaching staff. Of course, the ultimate team goal is to win! However, the chances of winning go up dramatically if the special teams perform at a high level.

Two separate "special teams goal" charts are illustrated in Tables 3-9 and 3-10. While the first chart is less complex than the second, it fits well with the "hidden-yards: The-game-within-the-game" form (Table 3-11). The phrase "hidden-yardage battle" is frequently used by coaches everywhere. This form gives the coach a concrete method of calculating whether the special teams are winning the hidden-yardage battle. To complete the "hidden yards" form, the coach must transpose the appropriate yardage from the kickoff, kickoff return, punt cover, and punt return "grading summary" forms. Then, he totals and averages the yardage to get plus or minus yards for these four kicking units. Any total plus yards should be considered a winning performance. A total plus yards of 20 yards or more is normally considered a dominating performance.

The second goal chart is more complex. The biggest contrast between it and the first goal chart example is the addition of general overall goals and big-play goals. If a big-play chart is not used, this goal chart is a good alternative to the first one.

Player Recognition and Awards

Many of the processes previously discussed in this chapter under "grading player performance and goals assessment" contribute to special teams player recognition. However, a coaching staff can do more to award outstanding special teams performance. The following discussion and examples illustrate how this objective can be achieved. For example, after each game, most coaching staffs typically discuss at least six aspects of their team's performance that impacted the outcome of the game. As a rule, these factors include:

- Short-yardage and goal-line success
- Assignment errors
- Penalties

- Turnovers/takeaways
- Big plays
- Kicking game

Table 3-9. A sample special teams goal chart.

SPECIAL TEAMS GOALS

SCHOOL
LOGO

Kickoff Coverage
Opponent Avg. Start Line- 25 YL

Kickoff Return
Avg. Start Line- 25 YL

Punt Coverage
Net 38 yards

Punt Pressure
Opponent Avg. 36 yards, Net, or
10 yard avg. return.

Block a punt

PAT/FG

100% PAT's

100% FG's within 40 yards

PAT/FG BLOCK

Block PAT or FG

Win the hidden Yards battle

Total hidden yards (+/-)

Win / Loss

Table 3-10. A more detailed sample special teams goals chart.

SPECIAL TEAMS GOALS

SCHOOL LOGO

General Overall Goals
1. Perfect substitution
2. No Penalties
3. No turnovers
4. No big plays allowed
5. Score or set up a score
6. Win hidden yards battle

General Overall Goals
1. Opp. avg. return
2. Opp. avg. start line
3. Tackle opp. inside the 20 yl.

Kickoff Return Goals
1. Average return
2. Avg. starting line

Punt Goals
1. Net punt
2. Gross punt
3. Opp. punt return avg.
4. Punt inside the 10 yds. line

Punt Pressure Goals
1. Punt return avg.
2. Avg. 36 yds. net or 10 yds. per return
3. Out return our opp. (avg./ret.)

Field Goal - PAT Goals
1. Make all FGs within 40 yds.
2. PAT:

Field Goal Block Goal
1. Force bad snap or kick
2. Block PAT or FG

Big Play Goals
1. Cause turnover
2. Block kick
3. KO return ASU 40 yl +
4. Punt return +20 yds.
5. Fake for 1st down or score
6. Stop fake or fire
7. Recover onside KO

Overall Totals

Win / Loss

Table 3-11. A sample special teams "hidden-yards: the game-within-the-game" form.

SPECIAL TEAMS

<u>Hidden Yards:</u>   "THE GAME WITHIN THE GAME"

	<u>KOC</u>	<u>KOR</u>	<u>PC</u>	<u>PR</u>
Goal	Avg. 25 YL	25 YL	38 Net	36 Net
Plays & +/-	1)	1)	1)	1)
	2)	2)	2)	2)
	3)	3)	3)	3)
	4)	4)	4)	4)
	5)	5)	5)	5)
	6)	6)	6)	6)
	7)	7)	7)	7)
	8)	8)	8)	8)
	9)	9)	9)	9)
	10)	10)	10)	10)

Avg.
Total +/- yds

       AVERAGE   **+/- YARDS**

KOC

KOR

PC

PR

TOTAL HIDDEN
YARDS

The kicking game, along with offense and defense, can be evaluated in all areas, except short yardage and goal-line success. The coach responsible for presenting an overview of the special teams performance to the staff should bring the "Special Teams Game Summary" form to this discussion (Table 3-12). In addition to the aforementioned aspects of play, this form provides space for the selection of three awards not previously discussed in this chapter:

- Special teams "Player of the Game" award
- The "Shoo Chicken" coverage award
- Kickoff coverage "Draw-the-Line" award

The criteria for selecting the special teams "Player of the Game" can vary from week-to-week, depending on what performance had the greatest impact on the outcome of the game. Generally, it should be awarded to a player who made positive contributions on several, if not all, of the kicking units. However, an outstanding performance by a kicker or kick returner could also be selected for this award. The selected player should be recognized along with the other award recipients.

The "Shoo Chicken" coverage award is given to a player or players who had multiple tackles on kickoffs and/or punt coverage. The "Special Teams Game Summary" form makes it easy to see which players had multiple tackles, because these particular stats are listed on the form.

The other special teams performance honor is the kickoff coverage "Draw the Line" award. This award is given to all players who are involved in a tackle inside the 20-yard line. To indicate all tackles, a kickoff coverage, draw-the-line chart (Table 3-13) can be posted with the names and tackles that are made by each player throughout the season. The player's jersey number is posted on the diagramed field at the spot of the tackle.

Where rules permit, it can also be beneficial and fun to award candy bars, t-shirts, shorts, caps, etc. for outstanding special teams performances. Not only should the logos be put on any clothing items that are given as awards in order to make them relevant and appropriate to the award, but also fun and appealing for the player to want to wear.

Table 3-12. A sample special teams game summary form.

SPECIAL TEAMS GAME SUMMARY

1. Special teams Player of the Game —

2. "Shoo Chicken" coverage Award

3. KOC Draw-the-Line ➜ 20 Award —

4. Big plays: <u>Our Team</u>   <u>Opponent</u>

5. Hidden yardage —

6. Tackles   <u>KOC   T/AT</u>   <u>PC   T/AT</u>

7. Penalties —

8. Assignment errors —

Table 3-13. A sample kickoff coverage draw-the-line chart.

KICKOFF COVER

DRAW THE LINE

#	Name	Tackle T/AT's

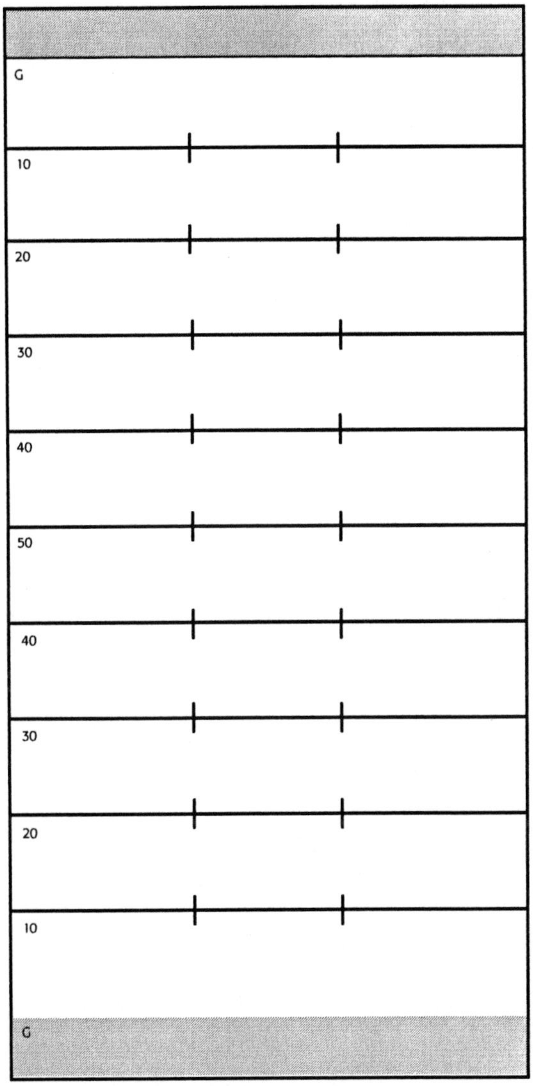

G
10
20
30
40
50
40
30
20
10
G

CHAPTER 4

PUNT PROTECTION AND COVERAGE

The next five chapters, in a playbook format, present a detailed discussion of the six special teams units—punt protection and coverage, punt return/block, kickoff cover, and kickoff return. PAT/field goal and PAT/field-goal defense are addressed in the same chapter.

In this chapter, two punt schemes are discussed — the spread punt and the tight punt. Each scheme has distinct advantages and disadvantages. The spread scheme allows the two wide "missiles" to get off the line of scrimmage and cover quickly to the returner. However, this scheme places more pressure on the snapper to not only deliver a perfect snap, but also to be involved in protection. On the other hand, the tight-punt scheme requires the ends to be involved in protection; thus, they are slower getting into coverage, particularly the "double-bump" end. Furthermore, because the snapper does not have a protection responsibility, he can concentrate fully on the snap.

THE MOST IMPORTANT PLAY IN FOOTBALL

No part of the kicking game can change the course of a game like the punting game. Nowhere in football is field position gained or lost as rapidly as it is in the punting game. On an average, each punt is worth 35-to-38 yards per exchange. This factor indicates why the punt is the "most important play" in football.

Regardless of the scheme used, the punting team's primary goal should be to net 38 yards per punt. This objective can be accomplished by several steps, including:

- Perfect snap
- Firm protection
- High-hanging punt
- Aggressive coverage
- Solid tackling

The punt team should adhere to the following general mechanics prior to the snap. In this regard, the punt team should:

- Always be ready on the sideline on third down.
- Huddle on the sideline for any special instructions.
- Hustle onto the field and get lined up without huddling.
- Take the proper split and stance and listen to the calls.
- See the ball with peripheral vision and move on the snap.
- Communicate clearly when necessary.

At the line of scrimmage, the punt team should perform the following procedures:

- The personal protector (PP or FB) should look to make sure there are eleven players on the field in proper position. He then makes a "ready" call to alert the team to listen to his calls.
- Initially, the PP/FB should make a front call, then a protection call.
- After the protection call, the punt team should communicate with each other if necessary.
- Next, the PP/FB should recheck the front before saying, "set." There can be no movement after the "set" call. The snapper should pause after "set", and then snap the ball.

The process of punting the ball involves the following four time elements:

- Center snap—the center must get the ball to the punter in .7 to .8 seconds. Any slower than this increases the risk of getting the punt blocked.
- Punters "in-hand time"—the punter must be able to get the ball off within 1.2 to 1.3 seconds on a two-step approach.
- Get-off time (combined snap time and in-hand time)—the elapsed time from snap-to-kick should be 1.9 to 2.1 seconds.
- Hang time (the time the ball is in the air)—the punter should strive to keep the ball in the air for 4.5 seconds to allow the coverage the opportunity to either keep the return to a minimum or force a fair catch.

The thought process chart shown in Table 4-1 illustrates the steps (in priority order) the punt team should go through in covering a punt of 40 yards. It is critically important that the players are drilled in the proper techniques and fundamentals required to perform all six of the steps outlined.

Table 4-1. A sample punt team thought process chart form.

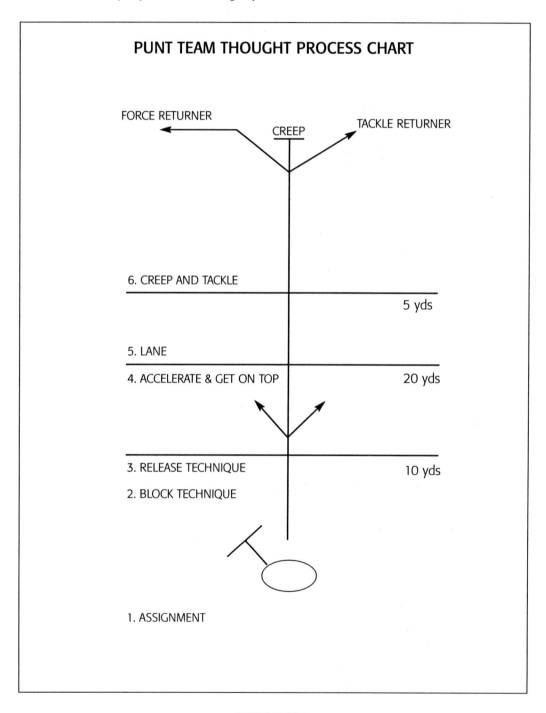

PRO-SPREAD PUNT

SPLITS AND ALIGNMENTS

FB
- Five-yards deep behind the guard.
- Stay at five-yards depth so he can check from the A-gap to the stress points.

X & Z (Missiles)
- The ball in the middle—split, halfway between the hash and the nine-yard slash.
- The ball on the hash and the wideside—split three yards outside the hash.
- The ball on the hash and the boundary side—nine yards from the sideline.

Wings
- Inside foot on the outside foot of the tackle, deep enough to keep the adjacent tackle from stepping on his inside foot on his first step.
- Outside foot back.

Guards
- Three-inch split between the snapper and them.
- Inside toe on the snapper's heels.
- Outside toe no deeper than the heel of their inside foot.

Tackles
- Six-inch split between the tackles and them.
- Inside toe on toe of the guard's outside foot.
- Outside toe no deeper than the heel of their inside foot.

Punter
- Heels 15-yards deep with his kicking foot directly behind the snapper's crack.

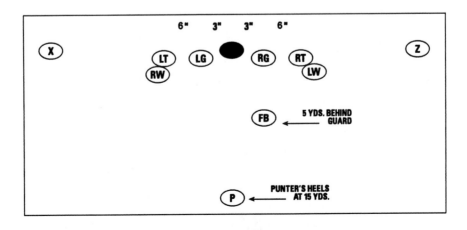

STANCE

All players take their two-point stance immediately upon reaching the LOS.

G's, T's and Wings — Hands lightly placed above their knees, head up, arch in their back, chin up, outside foot back, feet shoulder-width apart, and able to see the ball.

X and Z (Missiles)— Wide receiver's stance; use the sideline official to check their alignment to the LOS.

LEFT PROTECTION CALL:

G's: "Kick-slide" zone protection technique. Their first step is straight back with the outside foot ("Kick"), then slide their inside foot straight back, maintaining a shoulder-width stance (be able to help the snapper vs. an A-gap rusher by punching him with the inside hand on the slide step). Then, take a second "kick slide" to get depth and be able to see their man. *No separation of technique* between him and the tackle. "Slam" his hands through his man. He is responsible for the #3 man on his side. Do not widen until he has executed the "kick-slide" twice to place him self in position to see twists and blitzers. Slam his hands through his man by keeping his shoulders and feet at a 45-degree angle to the LOS. He must *not* "step in the bucket" and allow vertical penetration by a rusher.

T's: "Kick-slide" protection technique. Same as the guards, except they are responsible for the #2 man on their side.

W's: "Kick-slide" protection technique. Same as the guard and tackle, except they are responsible for the #1 man on their side.

SNAPPER: Perfect snap, then deepen and widen to the left side and "slam" his hands through the left side #4. Be alert for #4 looper (from the left- side A-gap to the right-side A-gap); he must then turn back toward the right-side A-gap and block the looper.

FB: Stay at five-yard depth as long as possible so he can check #4 on the right side to see if he is rushing or not. If #4 doesn't rush, this will enable the FB to check any "stress points." Versus an A-gap looper, he may have to double-bump if the snapper misses him.

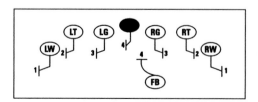

Diagram 4-1. Picking up twists and stack blitzes.

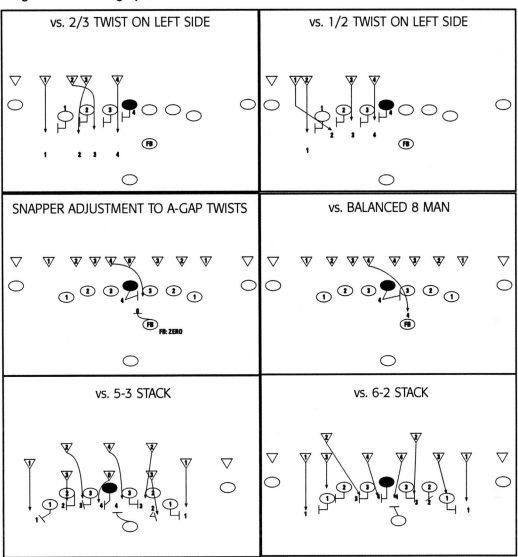

Diagram 4-2. Man protection calls.

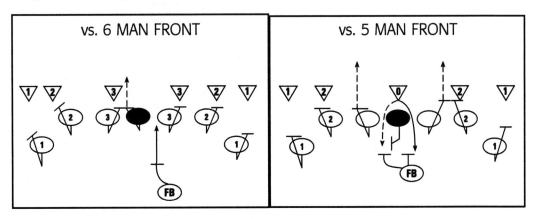

Diagram 4-3. "Check" zone protection calls.

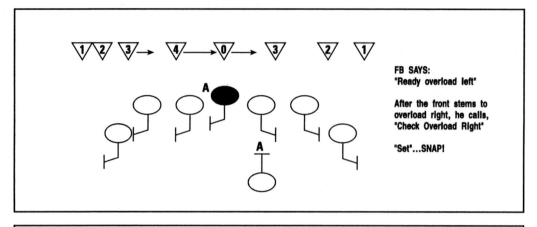

FB SAYS:
"Ready overload left"

After the front stems to
overload right, he calls,
"Check Overload Right"

"Set"...SNAP!

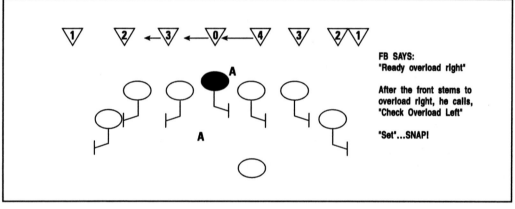

FB SAYS:
"Ready overload right"

After the front stems to
overload right, he calls,
"Check Overload Left"

"Set"...SNAP!

Diagram 4-4. "Quick snap" call.

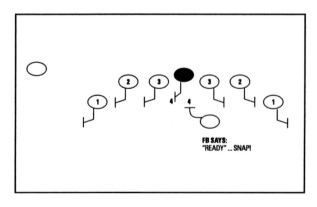

FB SAYS:
"READY" ... SNAP!

Diagram 4-5. The coach getting his team ready to go into the game on a "quick snap" sideline call.

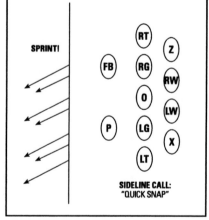

Diagram 4-6. Examples of commonly employed 8-man-fronts.

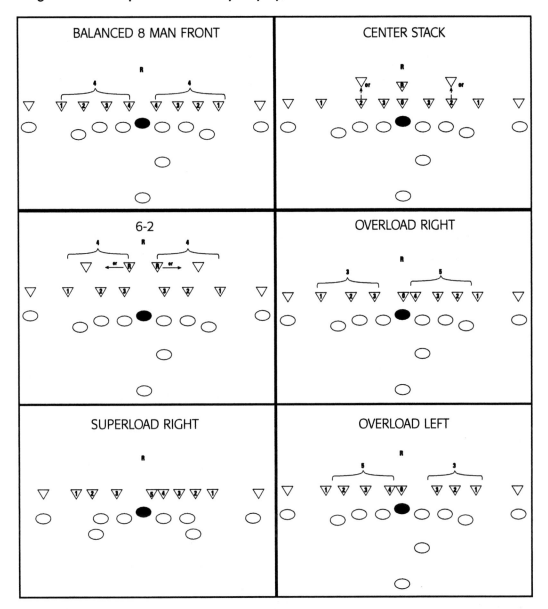

TITE PUNT ADJUSTMENT BETWEEN THE 5-YD. LINE AND THE GOAL LINE

A team that has to punt out of its own end zone is one of the most critical game situations it must face. The punt team must execute flawlessly and net at least 40 yards on the punt.

- Normal procedures, protection, coverage, and principals apply (no man calls). However, a "quick snap" may be called in this situation. All punt team personnel must know the situation and the call before taking the field.

- The missiles slam the end man on the LOS through his inside numbers, and then cover to the ball.

- The FB must *never line-up deeper than three yards from the goal line and never back-up after the snap*. The FB should remind the punter to align at least one foot from the end line before setting the punt team with a"ready call".

PUNTER'S ASSIGNMENTS:

- Align back foot at least one foot from the end line to avoid stepping on it while catching the snap.

- Two-step kick delivery.

- Know the situation so that he can make the correct decision regarding whether or not to take an intentional safety if bad snap occurs.

PUNT COVERAGE PRINCIPLES:

- Covering punts is based on SPRINTING after you block and release.

- SPRINT in your lane to cover. Never follow your own color jersey.

- Gang tackle. Force fumbles. Keep your shoulders parallel.

- Call out "FAIR CATCH" if one is signaled, give the returner two yards to catch the punt.

- On a fair-catch signal, converge early and get in the returner's face—expect a fumble (stay two yards away from him)!

- Know where the ball is. DO NOT let it hit you!

- If you have a free release, call "switch" to the next man inside and cover directly to ball.

- The returner's position should also give you a good idea where the ball will land.

- Get an "easy" release.

- Never get held up at the LOS on your release.

- Initially, the coverage should fan "wide" to cover the field, and then gradually converge on the ball.

Diagram 4-7. Tite punt (LOS between the 5-yd. line and the goal line.

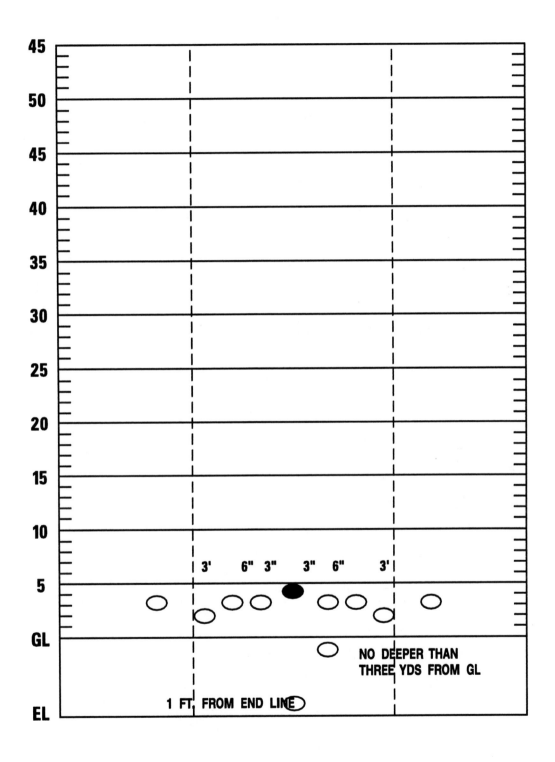

- "Missiles"—maintain outside leverage. Don't break down unless the returner gives a fair catch signal. Time-up your hit—take a shot at the returner's outside leg. Cause a turnover! Reroute the returner if you can't make tackle. If the receiver does not field the ball, you may "catch it" (sky punt). On a sky punt, if the receiver "fair catches", the first missile down should close, but not interfere with the catch. Are responsible for a dropped ball!

- Always give the returner two yards to catch the football.

- Tackle with intent to force a fumble.

- On a SKY KICK, defend the end zone—keep the ball from going in.

- Keep in mind that the punt coverage is a team effort—it takes eleven people to do the job.

- Make up your mind—you must sprint 40 yards to cover—PRIDE!!

- Be alert as to where the return is forming. Look for a "pre-set" wall.

- Study film. Know the tendencies of your opponent's returner and the types of returns that your opponent utilizes.

- Objectives of coverage:

  ❑ Force either a fair catch or no return at all.

  ❑ Hold the opposition to less than three yards per return.

  ❑ Cause a returner to fumble and recover the ball.

- The secret to good coverage is DESIRE.

- BLOCK – RELEASE – SPRINT - FAN OUT - TACKLE - FORCE - TURNOVER.

PUNT COVERAGE ASSIGNMENTS:

X and Z (Missiles):   Fast release and cover straight to the ball.

Snapper: Perfect snap. Cover straight to the ball. Mirror the ball and "Shoo Chicken."

Punter: Must make the returner run at lease 10 yards to catch ball. Make him move so he cannot locate the missiles.

FB: Cover to the ball. Mirror the returner. Game plan to cover either to the right or left vs. wall returns.

Guards: Release and maintain a lane five yards outside the ball. Stay square and keep the ball on their inside shoulder—"Shoo Chicken" (FILL).

Tackles:	Release outside for width and maintain a lane 10 yards outside the ball. Stay square and force the ball back inside—"Shoo Chicken." Never allow the ball to get outside them (FORCE).
Wings:	Release outside for width and maintain a lane 15 yards outside the ball. If the returner tries to get outside, bounce outside and keep ball on their inside shoulder. If the returner takes the ball up the field, fold from outside-in and make the tackle with their inside shoulder (BOUNCE-FOLD). Note: By game plan, the wing can exchange coverage assignment with the tackles.

Diagram 4-8. Pro spread coverage assignments.

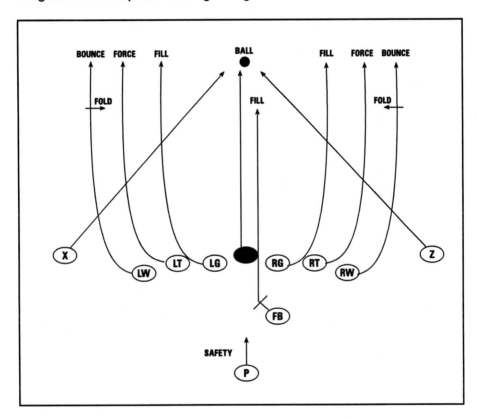

SKY & POOCH KICK—LEFT OR RIGHT—COVERAGE ASSIGNMENTS:

NOTE: You may catch the ball if your opponent does not attempt to. You must down the football on the field of play, preferably inside the 10-yard line.

CENTER: Snap and cover straight to the ball. On a "fair catch" signal, break down two yards from the returner.

MISSILES: The first man down should run by the returner and turn his back to the goal line. If the returner doesn't attempt to catch the ball, he can "catch it." The second man down should break down two yards from the returner. If the returner drops the ball, he should recover it.

SLOW COVERAGE: Same coverage responsibilities as normal, except be alert on a "fair catch" to recover a fumble or muff. Converge and squeeze early on a "fair catch."

PUNTER: Kick the ball high and have it land on the 10-yard line. Make the returner make a decision. Call out the direction of kick. He is the safety.

FULLBACK: Mirror the football. He is the safety. Echo the direction call.

Diagram 4-9. Sky and pooch coverage assignments.

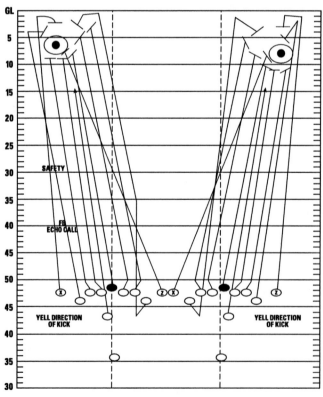

PUNTER'S CHECKLIST:

- Normal punt – 15 yards deep.

- Feet pointed straight ahead. Kicking foot in the snapper's crack.

- Concentrate on the snap from the center. Catch the ball with two hands. Take two steps!

- Place the ball correctly on the foot. (Perfect drop every time.)

- Follow-through.

- Cover and "shout" the the direction of the the kick (e.g., "right", "left", "middle", or "short").

- Know what yard line he is on for a "sky" or pooch (i.e.,corner) punt.

- Strive for height and accuracy. (Near the 50—sky punt on the 10-yard line.)

- Fourth down – punt the ball at all costs.

- Third down or quick kick – bad snap or fumble, recover the ball at all costs; DO NOT PUNT.

- A blocked kick behind the line of scrimmage can be advanced by both the kicking team and the return team. Be prepared to recover the ball or to tackle opponent.

- When in the end zone and a bad snap occurs:

  - ❏ If a safety will beat you, punt the ball at all costs. (Particularly, late in fourth quarter).

  - ❏ If a safety will tie, give them the safety. rather than a chance to recover a blocked punt for a touchdown or gain the ball near the goal line.

  - ❏ If ahead by three to eight points, take the safety.

  - ❏ When giving up a safety, run out of the end zone to avoid a fumble.

- Always keep the kicking tempo the same. EXCEPTION: Early pressure, tite punt situations.

- Always know the wind direction.

- Know the direction call on pooch kicks.

X AND Z (MISSILES) RELEASES

One-on-one Releases. This release is the same as when a wide receiver is running a route on a pass and the defender is in a bump-and-run (press) situation. Speed off the LOS is the missles' most important asset. See the ball snapped, but know where the defender is aligned. Always outrun a single coverage man. Try to split a double team, either at the LOS or upfield. Come out of their two-point stance low with their arms pumping.

- Release vs. an inside or outside press:

    ❑ Come out of your stance low and fast with arms pumping.

    ❑ Aim for a spot two yards opposite the side on which the defender is aligned (can also use a rip move with the arm nearest the defender).

    ❑ Outrun him to the ball!

    ❑ If he cuts you off before you can get on top of him, use a push-swim move to get vertical. A push swim move involves the following steps: move the foot opposite the direction you want to go; as your foot hits the ground, plant, and push off of it. At the same time, drive your opposite hand into the defender's back, using him as leverage. Swing the other arm over and push off him.

- Release vs. head up press:

    ❑ Bring your feet to balance quickly.

    ❑ Use an arm-over/swim technique (push-swim).

    ❑ Push or slap the defender's hands away from your body with the opposite hand of your swim technique.

    ❑ Can also head fake and swim him.

    ❑ Once you get up-field, make sure you have *outside* leverage on ball.

- Down-the-line release vs. press:

    ❑ Your first step should be flat down the LOS with your inside foot, followed by a crossover.

    ❑ Plant your third step, dip your upfield shoulder and drive hard and fast up the field. Try to get your hips past the defender's hips.

    ❑ Once you get upfield, make sure you have outside leverage on the ball.

Two-on-one releases. This release involves a situation where the missile is being double-teamed. The success of your release has a lot to do with your level of quickness, and speed and the position of the two defenders. You can use any of the previously described releases. However, there are also several other techniques that can be used vs. the double-team, including:

- Split the double-team (the defender positioned either side of you):

  ❏ Drive hard and fast at the center point of the two defenders.

  ❏ Keep your shoulders low.

  ❏ As you get to the middle of the two defenders, dip your inside shoulder and rip through to *daylight*.

  ❏ As you get through, accelerate upfield. If one man cuts you off, he will open up that side of the double-team. Use the push-swim technique to beat him to that side.

- Beating the leap-frog technique (to get back in direction of coverage lane):

  ❏ If forced away from your coverage lane upfield, look for daylight between the two defenders. Split the two defenders and accelerate upfield, keeping outside leverage on the ball.

  ❏ Outside lane to the ball – inside release – split the double-team to get outside.

  ❏ Inside lane to the ball – outside release – split the double-team to get inside.

SKY PUNT COVERAGE:

- Down the ball inside the 10-yard line.
- Recover a dropped ball.
- Don't let the ball bounce back toward the LOS.
- Catch the ball inside the 10-yard line on the "big hop".
- Catch a "fly ball" inside the 10-yard line when the returner doesn't attempt to catch it.
- First missile down – get behind the returner with back to the goal line.
- Second missile – front-up the returner and fall on a dropped ball (you must give him two-yard free catch zone – "cone of silence").

"NORMAL" SPREAD PUNT

STANCE:

- Place the hands on the knees.

- Keep the eyes on the ball.

- Position the inside toe on the center's heel.

- Square Stance by the up-backs and the fullback.

- The end on the defensive back's side should have his inside foot back, offset toward the "man-side".

- The end on the man side should use the same stance as the guard and the tackle.

Diagram 4-10. Splits and alignment on a normal punt.

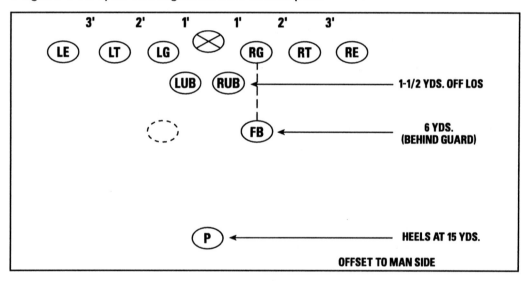

Diagram 4-11. Stance and foot placement on a normal punt.

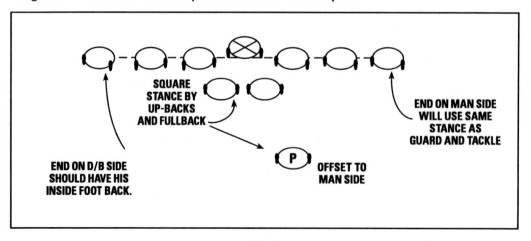

"MAN"-SIDE COMMUNICATION:
(No pointing unless absolutely necessary – talk to each other)

- The FB gives a "front" call, e.g., "balanced 10-Man", and a "direction" call.

- The guard begins his count, looks for the fourth man, and calls his number.

- The tackle blocks the next man outside of the guard's man.

- The end will tell the FB if he will block #1, #2, or #0 (a signal that refers to "I'm gone"), depending on the alignment (he will usually block #2; a "0" call will be rare).

- If any movement or stacks occur, the fullback may check to "Zorro" (zone).

- The center should lean toward the ZONE SIDE.

- The FB will then say, "SET,".........................snap!

Diagram 4-12. "Rosie " call.

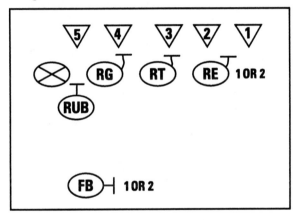

Diagram 4-13. "Louie" call.

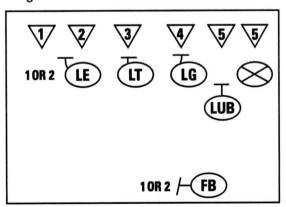

"ZONE-SIDE" PROTECTION:

LG: Align one foot from center (your inside toe on the center's heel). Anchoring your inside foot in place, pointing straight ahead, step outside behind the tackle's foot. Slam the zone outside of you, keeping your chest over your outside knee. You are responsible for the outside gap. Your inside foot will help the up-back. Keep the heel of your anchor foot on the ground (i.e., "ANCHOR-SLAM" TECHNIQUE).

LT: Align two feet from the guard (your inside toe on center's heel). Use "ANCHOR-SLAM" technique. Your block to the outside gap is critical to the end who has a "DOUBLE-BUMP" responsibility.

LE: Align three feet from the tackle, your inside foot back! Step back with your inside foot first. Backpedal to the "block point." Defend the "block point with a double-bump" technique, if necessary. NOTE: If one man heads up to the outside, the LE should block man. If two or more men head up to outside, he should "double bump".

LUB: Align in the "A" gap as close to the LOS as possible, while being legally in backfield. Step up with your inside foot first. Block the entire gap (i.e., "plug" technique).

FB: You will only "help" on the ZONE side if you make a "solid" call.

Diagram 4-14. "Rosie" call.

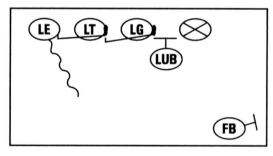

Diagram 4-15. "Louie" call.

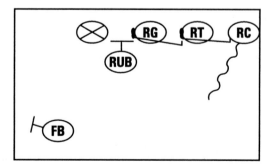

"ZORRO" PROTECTION:

In "ROSIE" or "LOUIE" protection, the call side of the protection is MAN and the other side is ZONE. If we either check to "ZORRO" on the LOS or call "QUICK ZORRO" on the sideline, both sides of the protection will be "ZONE", with the exception of the backside end and fullback; they will stay with the "ROSIE" or "LOUIE" responsibilities called on the sideline.

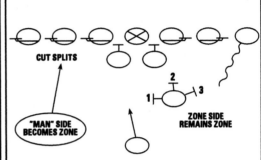

Diagram 4-16. "Zorro Rosie" call.

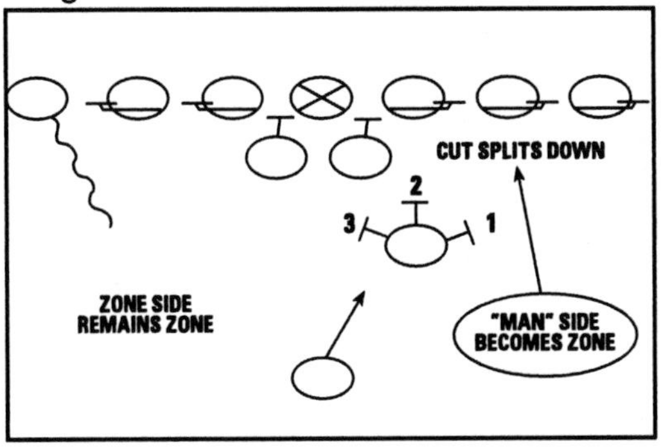

Diagram 4-17. "Zorro-Louie" call.

"QUICK – ZORRO – ROSIE":

When the objective is to have the ball snapped quickly, the call on the sideline will be: "QUICK ZORRO ROSIE." This means that the punt team will:

- Get aligned quickly on the LOS.

- Listen for a "ready" call by the FB.

- Watch the ball for a *quick snap.*

Diagram 4-18. "Quick-Zorro-Rosie" call.

Diagram 4-19. The coach getting his team ready to go into the game on a "Quick-Zorro-Rosie" sideline call.

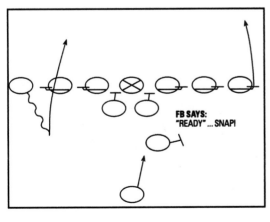

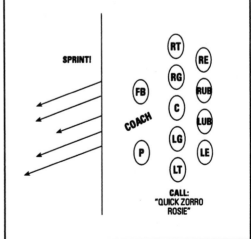

10-MAN FRONT
RECOGNITION OF DEFENSIVE ALIGNMENTS

Diagram 4-20. Examples of commonly employed 10-man front defensive alignments.

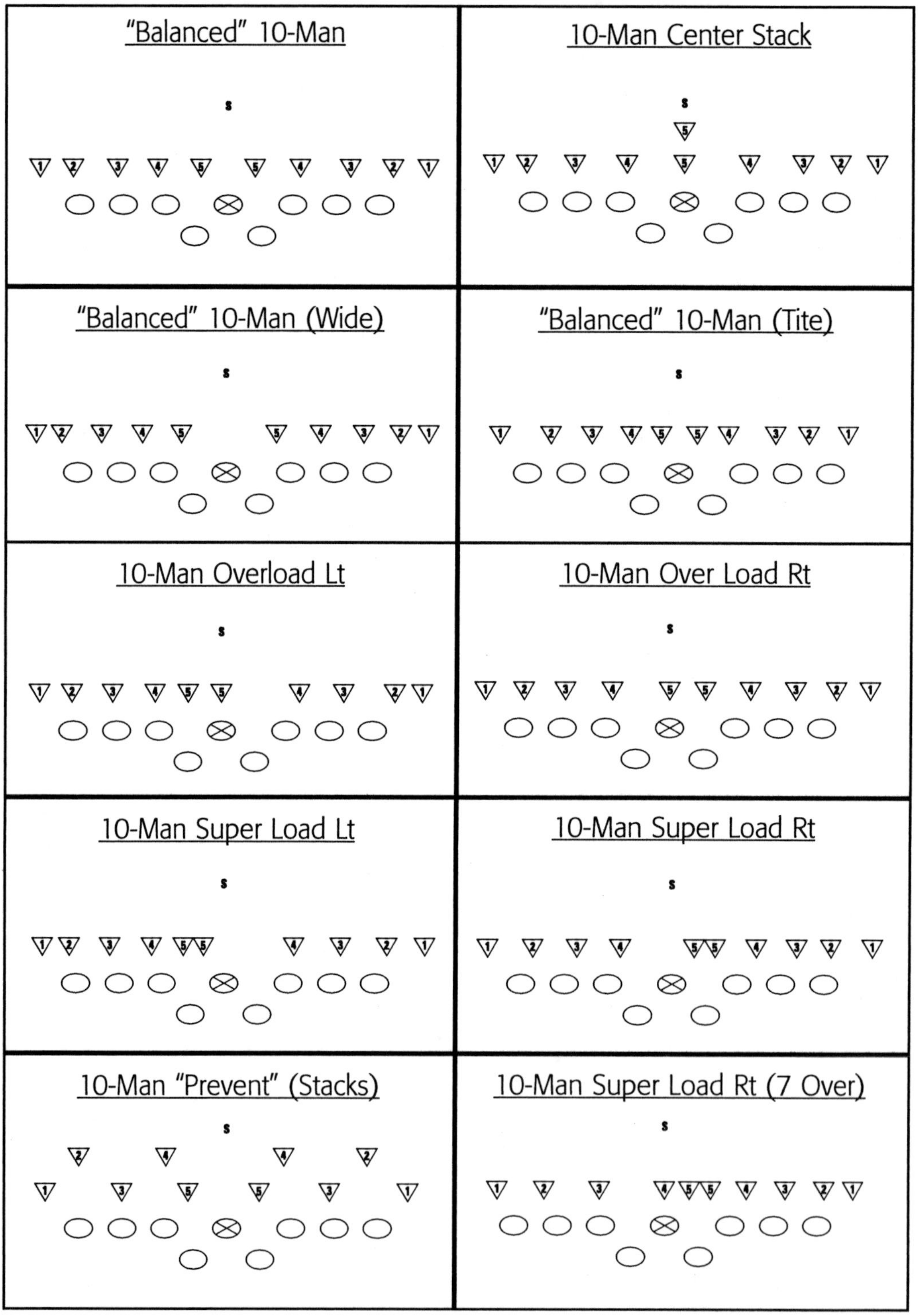

Diagram 4-21. "Rosie" and "Louie" vs. 10-man fronts.

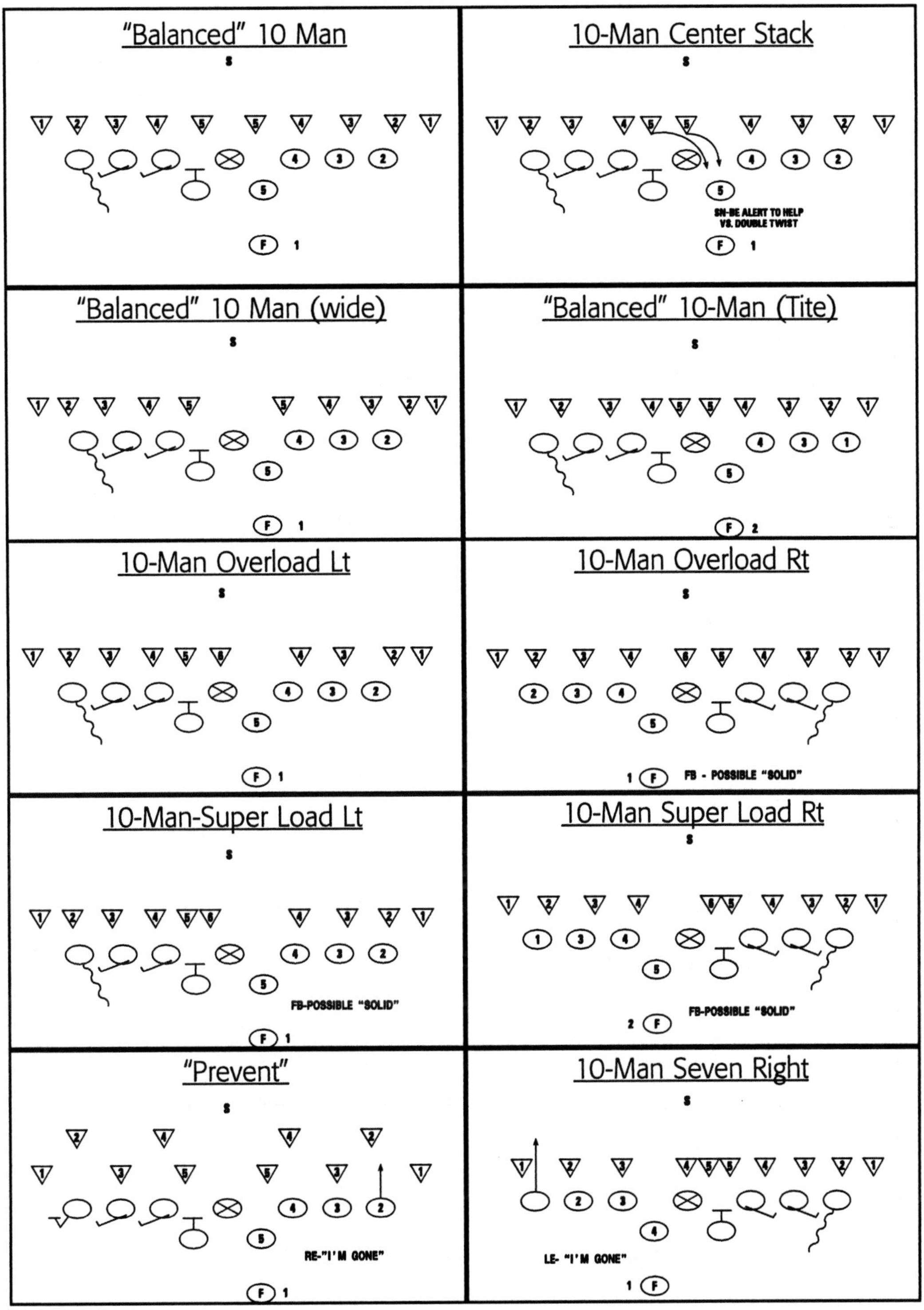

"Balanced" 10 Man

10-Man Center Stack

SN-BE ALERT TO HELP VS. DOUBLE TWIST

"Balanced" 10 Man (wide)

"Balanced" 10-Man (Tite)

10-Man Overload Lt

10-Man Overload Rt

FB - POSSIBLE "SOLID"

10-Man-Super Load Lt

10-Man Super Load Rt

FB-POSSIBLE "SOLID"

FB-POSSIBLE "SOLID"

"Prevent"

10-Man Seven Right

RE-"I'M GONE"

LE- "I'M GONE"

Diagram 4-22. "Solid" call adujustments vs. 10-man fronts.

Note: The "solid" call vs. overloads is the preferred adjustment because it allows man protection on one side.

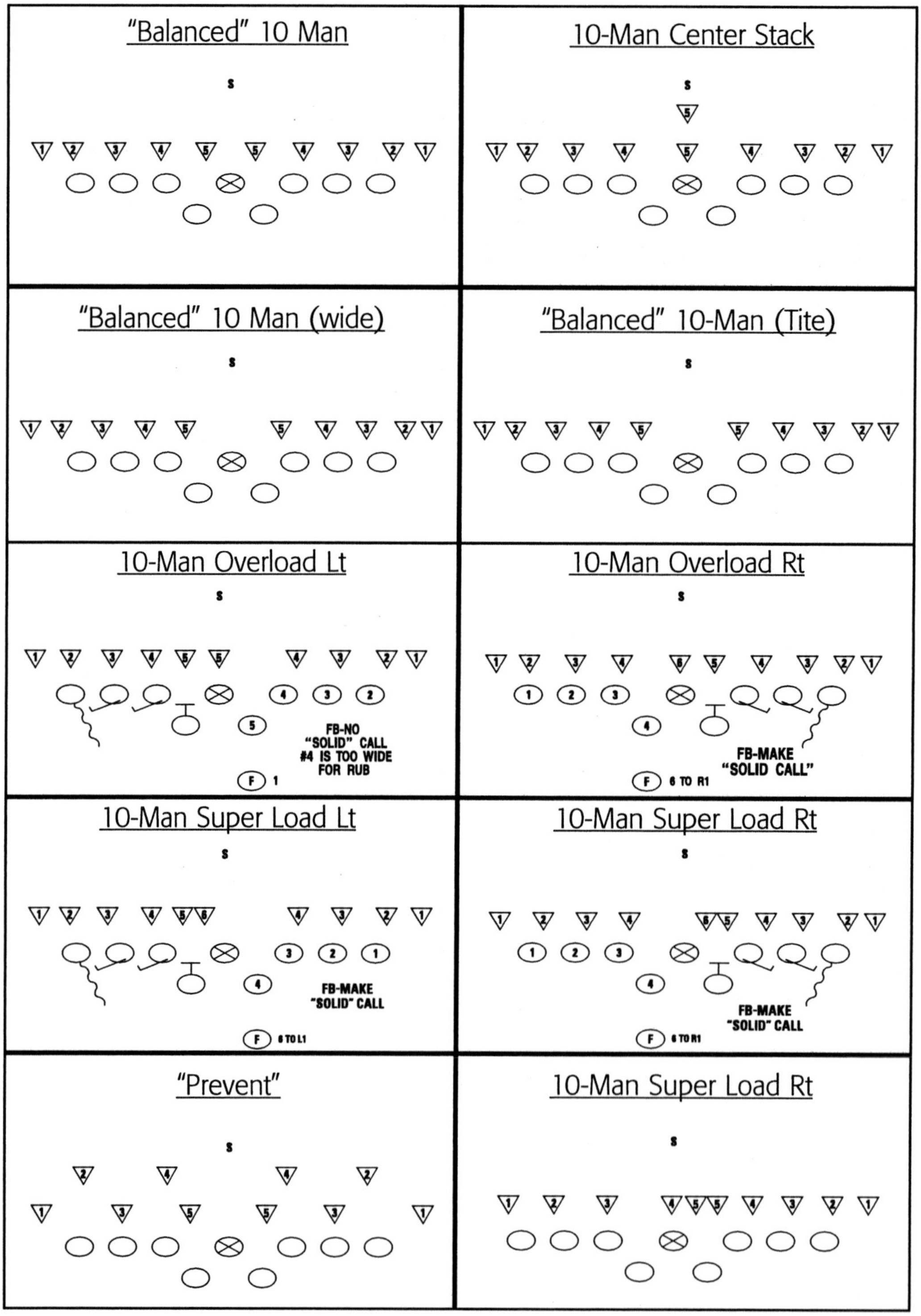
"Balanced" 10 Man
10-Man Center Stack
"Balanced" 10 Man (wide)
"Balanced" 10-Man (Tite)
10-Man Overload Lt
FB-NO "SOLID" CALL #4 IS TOO WIDE FOR RUB
F 1
10-Man Overload Rt
FB-MAKE "SOLID CALL"
F 6 TO R1
10-Man Super Load Lt
FB-MAKE "SOLID" CALL
F 6 TO L1
10-Man Super Load Rt
FB-MAKE "SOLID" CALL
F 6 TO R1
"Prevent"
10-Man Super Load Rt

ADJUSTMENTS FOR TROUBLE FRONTS

Diagram 4-23. Examples of adjustments to trouble fronts.

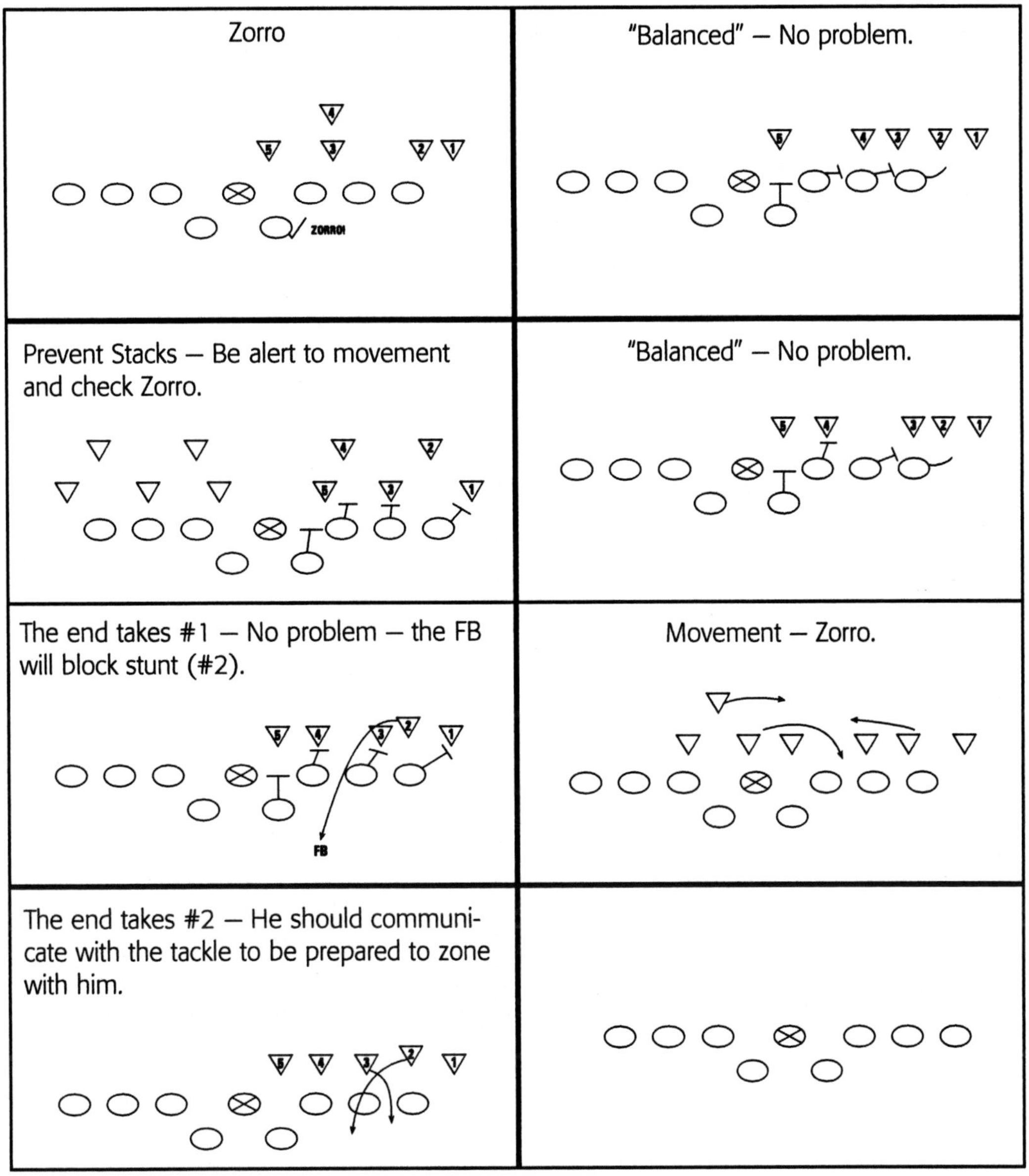
Zorro
ZORRO!
"Balanced" – No problem.
Prevent Stacks – Be alert to movement and check Zorro.
"Balanced" – No problem.
The end takes #1 – No problem – the FB will block stunt (#2).
FB
Movement – Zorro.
The end takes #2 – He should communicate with the tackle to be prepared to zone with him.

COVER "1 OR 2" ASSIGNMENTS:

(EXAMPLE – "ROSIE")

CENTER: Perfect snap. Cover straight to the ball. Mirror the ball.

ENDS: On either a "ROSIE" or "LOUIE" call, he has a *"BALL"* responsibility in coverage (after he blocks). Make the hit on his inside shoulder.

FULLBACK: Mirror the football. Echo the direction call of the punt. He is an aggressive safety.

PUNTER: Give the direction call of the punt. Keep the ball in front of him at all times. He is the *safety*!

Diagram 4-24. Cover 1 or 2 assignments on a "Rosie" call.

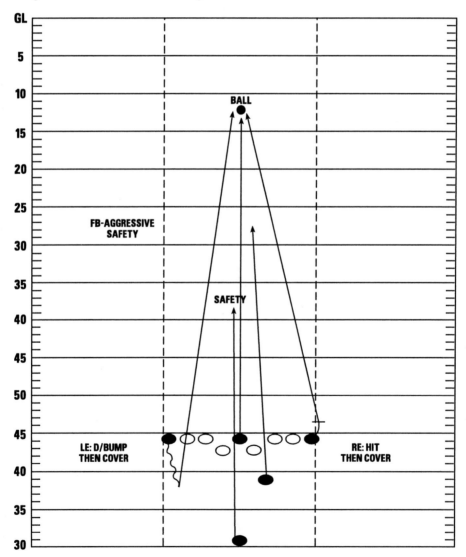

COVER "1 OR 2" ASSIGNMENTS:

(EXAMPLE – "LOUIE")

CENTER: Perfect snap. Cover straight to the ball. Mirror the ball.

ENDS: On either a "ROSIE" or a "LOUIE" call, he has a *"BALL"* responsibility in coverage (after he blocks). Make the hit on his inside shoulder.

FULLBACK: Mirror the football. Echo the direction call of the punt. He is an *aggressive* safety.

PUNTER: Give the direction call of the punt. Keep the ball in front of him at all times. He is the *safety*!

Diagram 4-25. Cover 1 or 2 assignments on a "Louie" call.

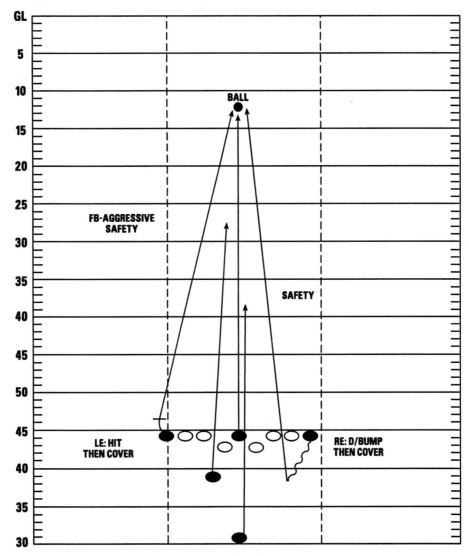

COVER "1" ASSIGNMENTS:

UP-BACKS: Release and maintain a lane five yards outside the ball. Stay square and keep the ball on his *inside* shoulder as he converges and squeezes the ball ("fill"). Ball away – become a "missile."

GUARDS: Release and maintain a lane 10 yards outside the ball. Stay square and keep the ball on his *inside* shoulder as he converges and squeezes the ball ("fill").

TACKLES: Release outside for width and maintain a lane 15 yards outside the ball. Stay square and force the ball back inside. *NOTHING GETS OUTSIDE – ("FORCE").*

Diagram 4-26. Cover 1 assignments.

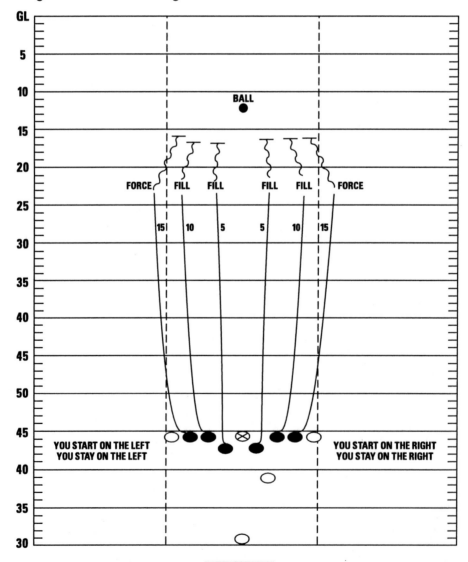

COVER "2" ASSIGNMENTS:

GUARDS: Release and maintain a lane five yards outside the ball. Stay square and keep the ball on his *INSIDE* shoulder as he converges and squeezes the ball. ("fill").

TACKLES: Release and maintain a lane 10 yards outside the ball. Stay square and keep the ball on his *INSIDE* shoulder as he converges and squeezes the ball. ("fill").

UP-BACKS: Release outside for width and maintain a lane 15 yards outside the ball. Stay square and force the ball back inside. *NOTHING GETS OUTSIDE—"FORCE".*

Diagram 4-27. Cover 2 assignments.

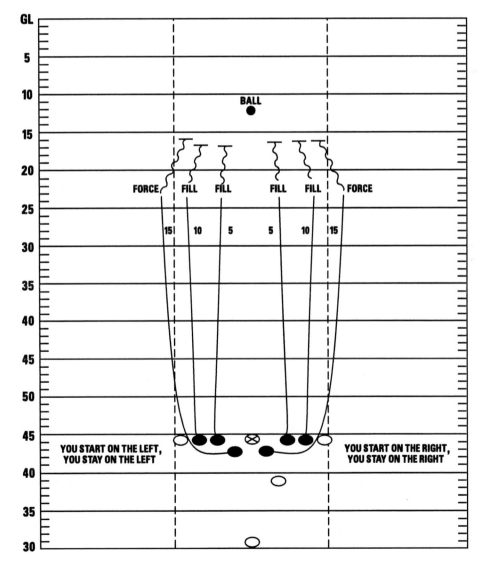

ASSIGNMENTS ON A SKY OR CORNER KICK SITUATION:

NOTE: You may catch the ball if your opponent does not attempt to so. You must down the football on the field of play, preferably inside the 10-yard line.

CENTER: Snap and cover straight to the ball. On a "fair catch" signal, break down two yards from the returner.

FAST COVERAGE: After they block, release straight to the ball. On "fair catch" signal, work by the return man *to the goal line.* Keep the ball from going into the end zone.

SLOW COVERAGE: Same coverage responsibilities as normal, except be alert on "fair catch" to recover a fumble or muff. *Converge and squeeze early* on "fair catch.

PUNTER: Kick the ball high and land it on the 10-yard line. Make the returner make a decision. Call out the direction of the kick. He is the safety.

FULLBACK: Mirror the football. He is the safety. Echo the direction call.

Diagram 4-28. Sky or corner kick assignments.

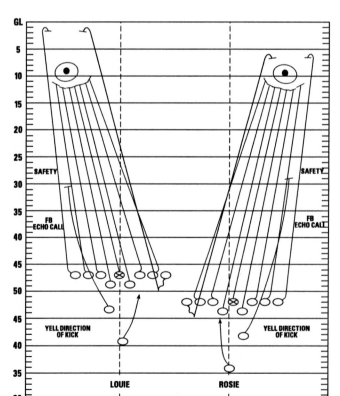

Diagram 4-29. A danger punt situation from a normal spread punt.

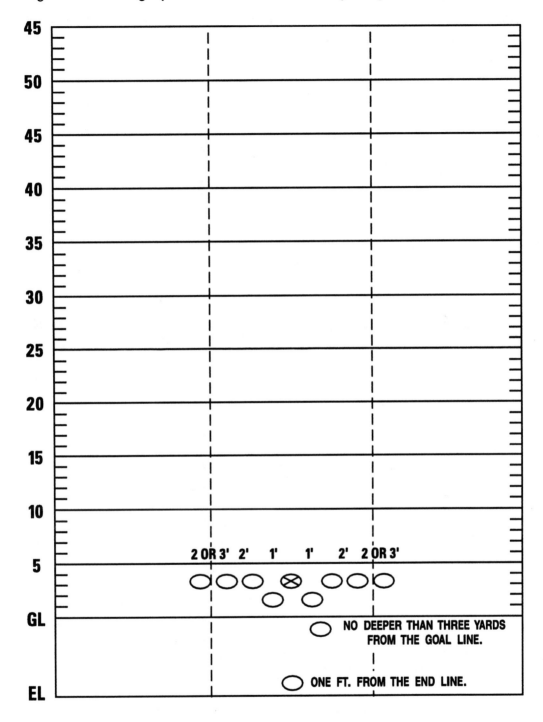

DANGER PUNT SITUATION BETWEEN THE FIVE-YARD LINE AND THE GOAL LINE

Punting out of its own end zone is one of the most critical game situations that a team can face. The punt team must execute flawlessly and net at least 40 yards on the punt.

- Normal procedures, protection and coverage principles apply. However, a "QUICK ZORRO ROSIE" may be called in this situation. All punt team personnel must know the situation and call before taking the field.

- The man-side end should reduce his split to two feet. The double-bump end should be alert to a tighter block point.

- The FB must never line-up deeper than three yards from the goal line and never backup after the snap. The FB should remind the punter to align at least one foot from the end line, before setting the punt team with a "ready call.

- The punter's assignments:

  - ❑ Align his back foot at least one foot from the end line to avoid stepping on the end line while catching the snap.

  - ❑ Employ a two-step kick delivery.

  - ❑ Know the situation so that he can make the correct decision regarding whether or not to take an intentional safety if a bad snap occurs.

CHAPTER 5

PUNT RETURN/BLOCK

A blocked kick or a return for a touchdown is one of the greatest momentum builders in football. Therefore, the punt return/block scheme should exert maximum effort to block the punt. The key factor is PRESSURE! While pressure will not block all punts, it will enable the punt coverage unit to block every punt where there is a flaw in the punting operation. And, if the punt is not blocked, great effort should be exerted to set the wall for a return. The basic concept is to take the wall to the ball—the closer to the sideline the better. On wall returns, the blockers must be dependable to block above the waist and in front.

Proper selection of personnel is the most important aspect of successful blocks/returns. And, dependability is the most important trait. In that regard, the punt coverage personnel should:

- Stay onside (see the ball snapped).

- Stay off the punter (unless you block the kick).

- Attempt to block above the waist and in front.

- Always pressure the punter and attempt to break his rhythm.

- Furthermore, the return man should catch all punts (i.e., do not let the ball hit the ground).

- Make the proper "fair catch" signal.

- Know the return call.

- Know that "Peter...Peter" means the ball is hitting the ground. Locate the ball and get away from it. The returner should also use a visual "wipe away" hand signal.

Since very few punt teams huddle on the field, the return/block team generally does not huddle. On third down, the return/block team members (not already in the game) should gather on the sideline for the call. As the sideline players take the field, they must communicate the call to the players on the field so everyone knows the call. When the line of scrimmage is near midfield, the sideline players must be alert for either a "SAFE" return (i.e., the defense stays on the field), or a regular return/block and mass substitute.

Blocking the punt involves four basic elements:

- Sprinters stance (bunch start):
    - ❑ One hand down, shoulders over the down hand.
    - ❑ Up hand on the thigh.
    - ❑ The butt higher than shoulders.
    - ❑ The feet narrow-width apart.
- Alignment:
    - ❑ "Credit card thin" to the LOS.
    - ❑ Each punt block team member's eyes on the ball.
    - ❑ The #1's look inside to make sure their side is onsides.
- Get-off:
    - ❑ "Grab grass" with the down hand.
    - ❑ The back foot replaces the down hand.
    - ❑ Keep the shoulders down.
    - ❑ Attack the opponent's inside leg; when he turns out, scrape to the block point.
- Block, scoop, and score:
    - ❑ The block point is two feet in front of punter's foot.
    - ❑ Extend the hands to the ball—always keep the hands below your chin.
    - ❑ Scoop and score.
    - ❑ If the punt block team doesn't get the block, they should turn, run, and take the wall to the ball.

The following thought-process chart illustrates the steps that the punt block team should go through in blocking a punt. It is important that players are drilled in the proper techniques and fundamentals required to perform all three of the steps outlined.

Table 5-1. The thought processes in blocking a punt chart.

THOUGHT PROCESSES IN BLOCKING A PUNT

15-YARDS DEEP	PUNTER
9-YARDS DEEP	STEP #3
	X BLOCK PUNT • KEEP EYES ON THE BALL • TAKE BALL OFF PUNTER'S FOOT X • STAY ON YOUR FEET WHEN POSSIBLE • SCOOP AND SCORE
6-YARDS DEEP	STEP #2
	PREPARATION POINT • SEE THE BALL • ELONGATE YOUR BODY • DO NOT SLOW UP • RUN THE HOOP
LOS	STEP #1
	• STANCE • GET OFF • DEFEAT THE BLOCK

Note: Start at the bottom and work up.

SCOUTING REPORT

One of the primary purposes of a team's scouting report should be to provide information about the opponent's punt formation on a weekly basis. However, it is important for the punt return/block unit to be able to recognize the various punt formations and determine who are the eligible receivers in each formation. (Refer to Diagram 5-1).

PUNT FORMATION RECOGNITION:

- "Normal" tite
- "Normal" flex
- "Spread"
- "Double wing"
- "Shield"

PUNT RETURNERS

In addition to teaching punt returners the fundamentals of catching punts, the coach should also communicate the following principles:

- They MUST catch all punts. Allowing a punt to roll on the ground loses valuable yardage (16 yards on the average).

- Know the return, blocking, etc.

- Be aware of the wind direction, sideline, and distance that the opponent can punt the ball.

- Always look to the bench for instructions.

- Make their fair catch signal a decisive one (i.e., wave one arm overhead twice).

- They don't have to catch a punt even though they have signaled for a fair catch. However, they cannot block after signaling for fair catch.

- If backed up deep in their own territory, set up on the 10-yard line. Handle all punts on or in front of the 10. If the ball is punted inside the 10, let it go, drawing the coverage away. If the ball is going into the end zone, be a good actor. Draw coverage to them, away from the ball.

- Score a touchdown or make a first down (i.e., achieve a 10-yard return or more).

- A "Peter…Peter" call—the term "Peter" means they do not want to touch the ball downfield. In certain prevent situations (i.e., on partially blocked punts and on shanked punts), they will often not want to risk fielding the ball. Make a "Peter...Peter" call and use a "wipe-away" hand signal to alert their own return team to get away from it. Let the ball roll.

- Know the rule of first touch. The official's whistle downs the ball.

- On a safe return with dual safeties, the safeties must communicate. The designated safety will make the calls. He will call, "Me-Me-Me" or "You-You-You." The man not making the catch must step in front of him. He must not be driven back into the catcher. He must advise the catcher when he should "fair catch" by yelling, "FAIR CATCH...FAIR CATCH."

Diagram 5-1. Common punt formations.

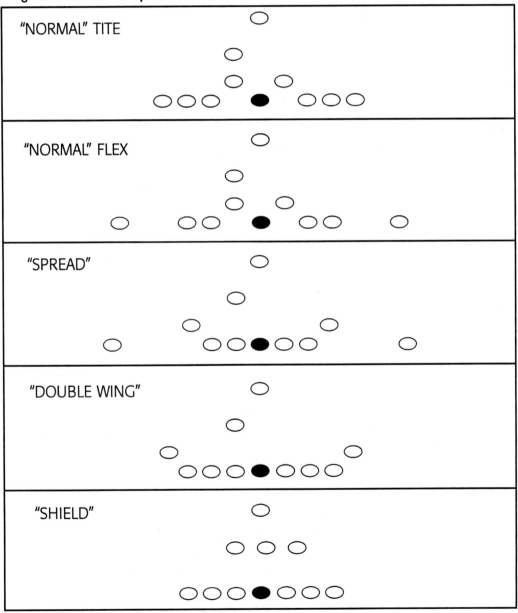

PUNT RETURNS AND BLOCKS VS. A SPREAD PUNT

Diagram 5-2. Middle return.

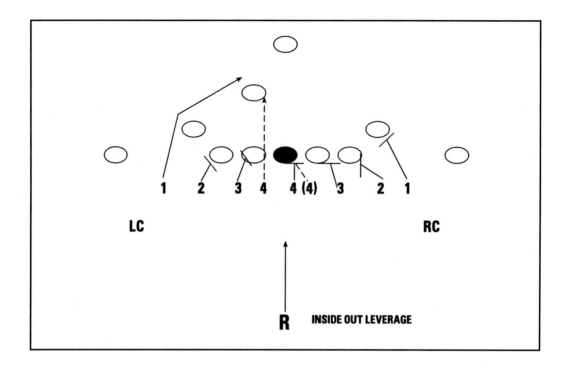

Diagram 5-3. Overload right—block right, return left.

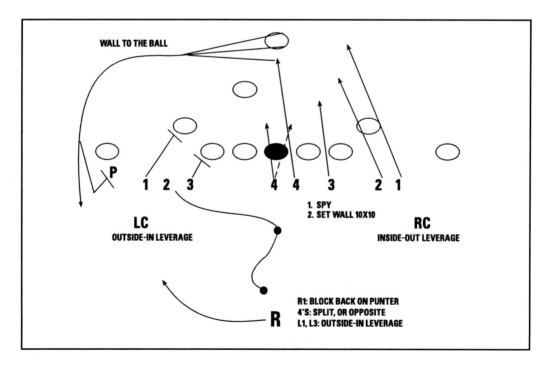

Diagram 5-4. Middle return with A-gap blocks.

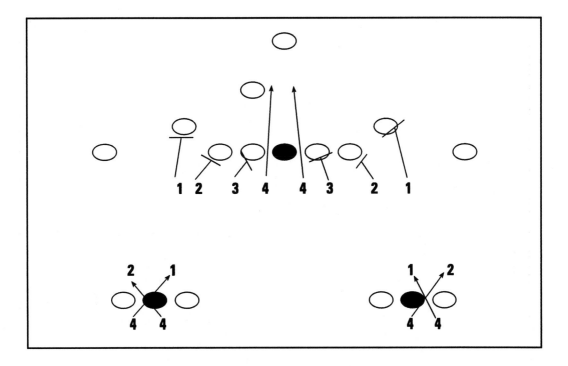

Diagram 5-5. Overload left—block left, return right.

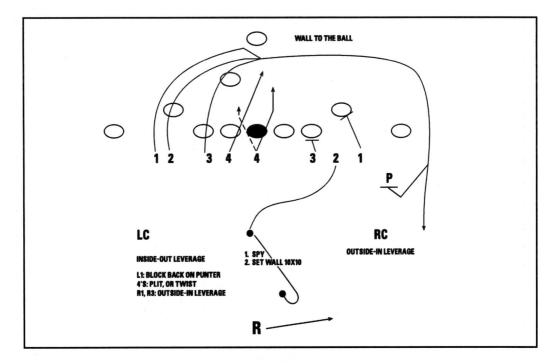

Diagram 5-6. 8-man block, return left. Automatic return left if don't block it.

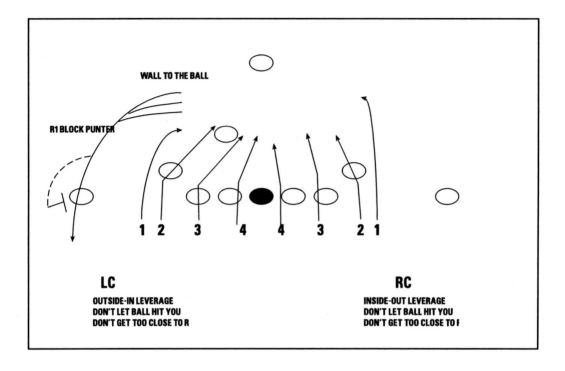

Diagram 5-7. 8-man block, return right. Automatic return right if don't block it.

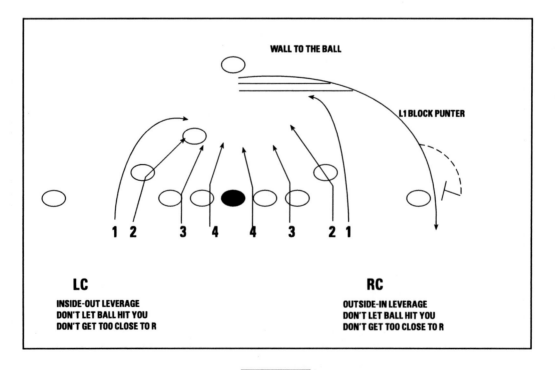

Diagram 5-8. 6-man block, return left.

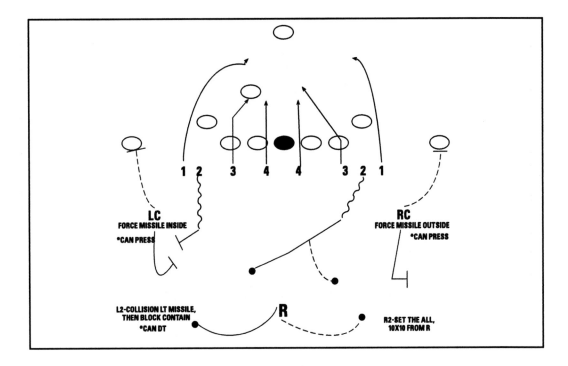

Diagram 5-9. 6-man block, return right.

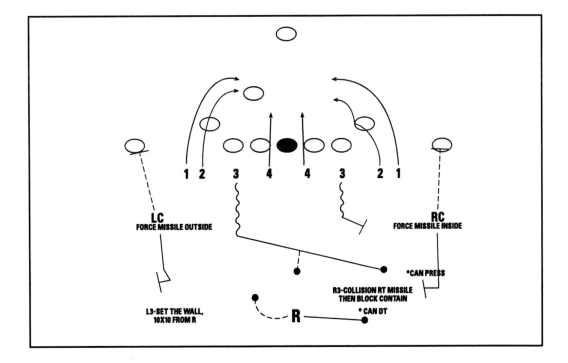

STACK CHANGE-UPS

Diagram 5-10. Examples of stack change-ups to confuse the snapper's and fullback's direction call.

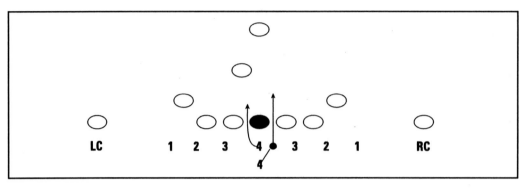

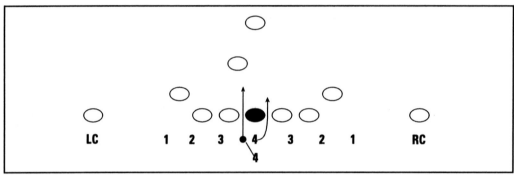

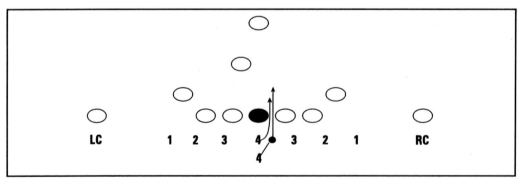

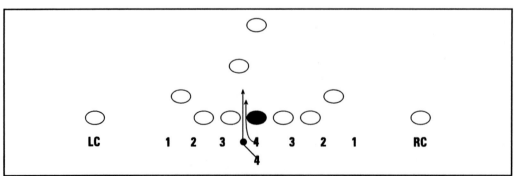

STEM CHANGE-UPS

Diagram 5-11. Examples of change-ups to confuse the snapper's and fullback's direction call.

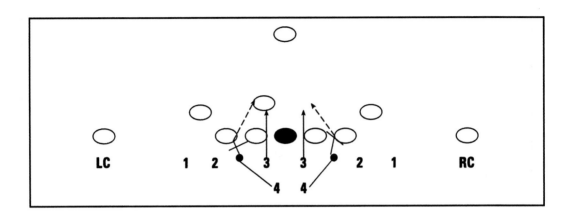

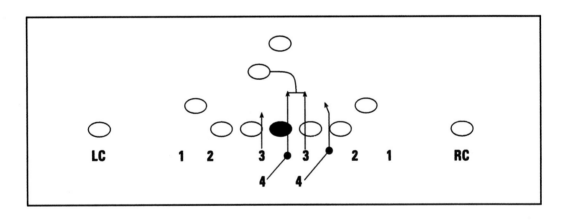

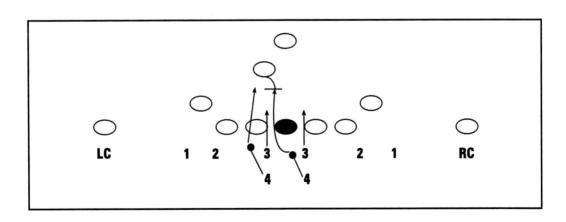

SCRAMBLE CHANGE-UPS

Diagram 5-12. Examples of change-ups to comfuse the snapper's and fullback's direction call.

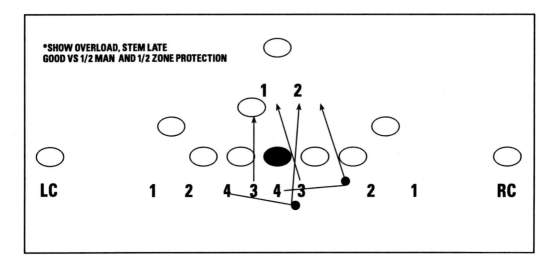

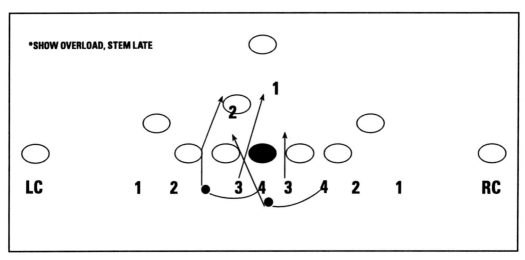

PUNT RETURNS AND BLOCKS VS. TITE PUNT

Diagram 5-13. Overload left, middle return.

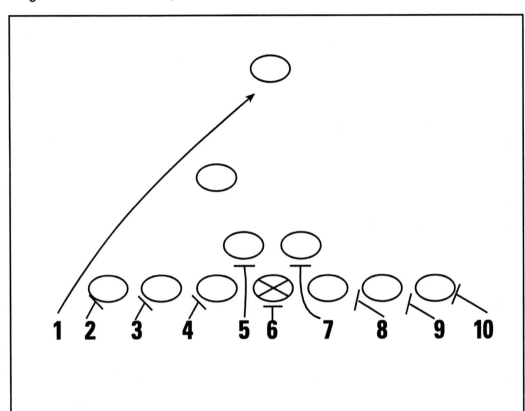

1   2   3   4   5   6   7   8   9   10

R

*INSIDE-OUT LEVERAGE

#6 & #7 CAN EXCHANGE ASSIGNMENTS TO GET A CROSS-BLOCK
NOTE: MIDDLE RETURN CAN ALSO BE RUN FROM OVERLOAD RIGHT

Diagram 5-14. Overload left, 10-man block, return right.

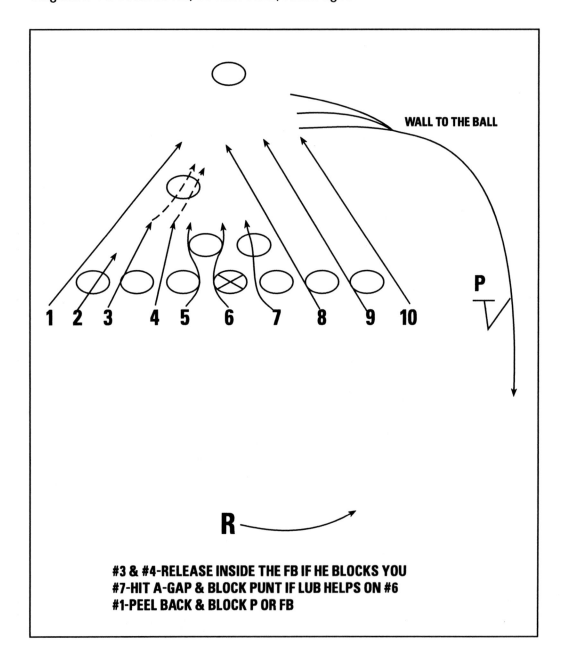

WALL TO THE BALL

1 2 3   4 5 6   7   8   9 10

P

R

#3 & #4-RELEASE INSIDE THE FB IF HE BLOCKS YOU
#7-HIT A-GAP & BLOCK PUNT IF LUB HELPS ON #6
#1-PEEL BACK & BLOCK P OR FB

Diagram 5-15. Overload left, block left, return right.

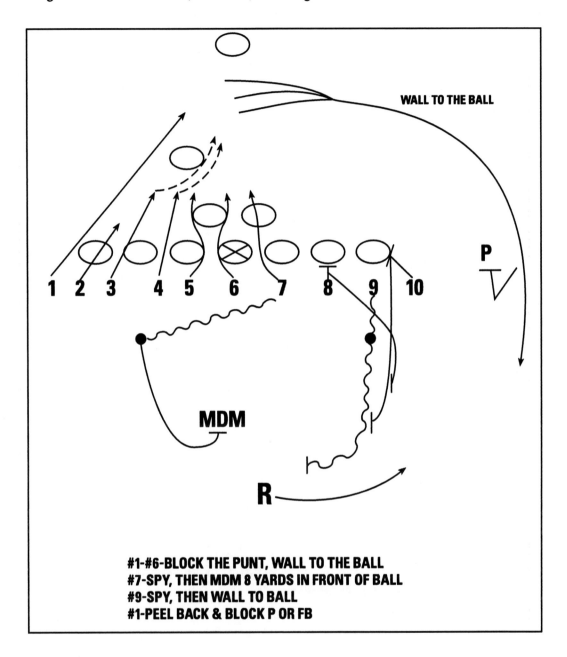

#1-#6-BLOCK THE PUNT, WALL TO THE BALL
#7-SPY, THEN MDM 8 YARDS IN FRONT OF BALL
#9-SPY, THEN WALL TO BALL
#1-PEEL BACK & BLOCK P OR FB

Diagram 5-16. Overload right, block right, return left.

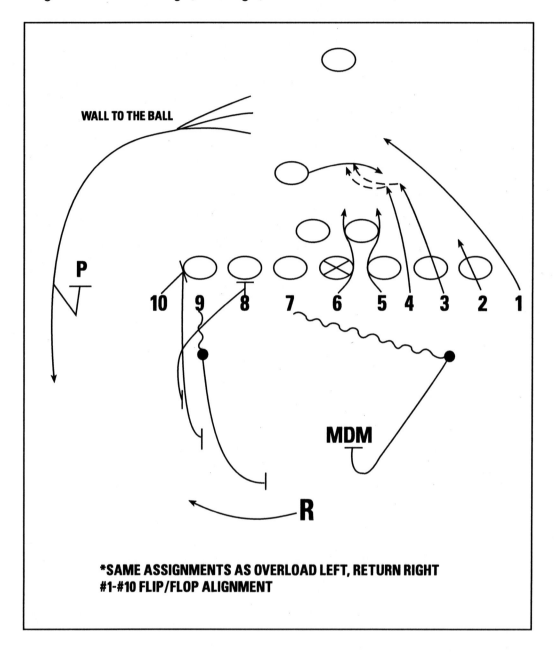

WALL TO THE BALL

P

10 9 8 7 6 5 4 3 2 1

MDM

R

*SAME ASSIGNMENTS AS OVERLOAD LEFT, RETURN RIGHT
#1-#10 FLIP/FLOP ALIGNMENT

"SAFE " PUNT RETURN (Note: expect a fake; employ "cover 2 man" coverage; use normal defensive personnel.)

Diagram 5-17. An example of a safe punt return.

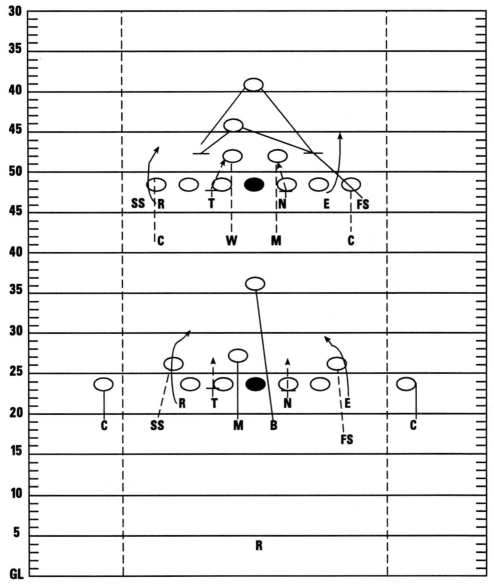

NOTE: THIS CALL ("SAFE") WILL BE USED BY THE "NORMAL DEFENSIVE PERSONNEL"—
SAM OUT! RETURNER IN!
IN FIELD-GOAL SITUATIONS ALSO.

COMMON PUNT "FAKES" FROM A TIGHT PUNT (Note: be alert.)

Diagram 5-18. Examples of fake punt plays from a tite punt formation.

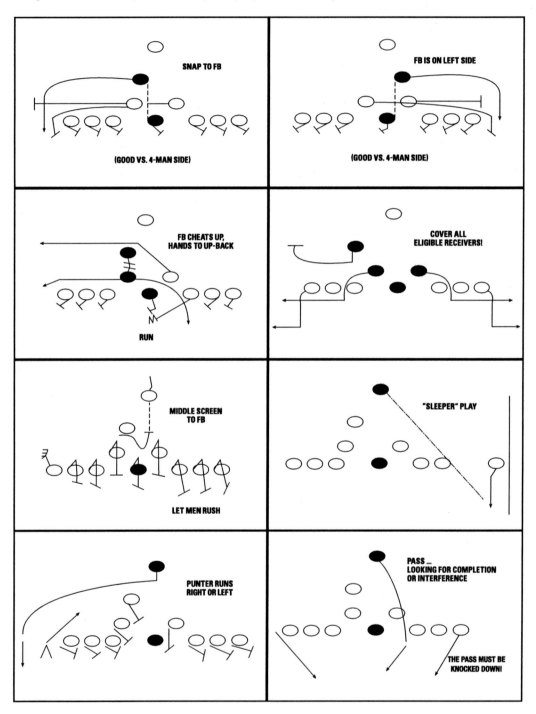

COMMON PUNT "FAKES" FROM A SPREAD PUNT

Diagram 5-19. Examples of fake punt plays from a special punt formation.

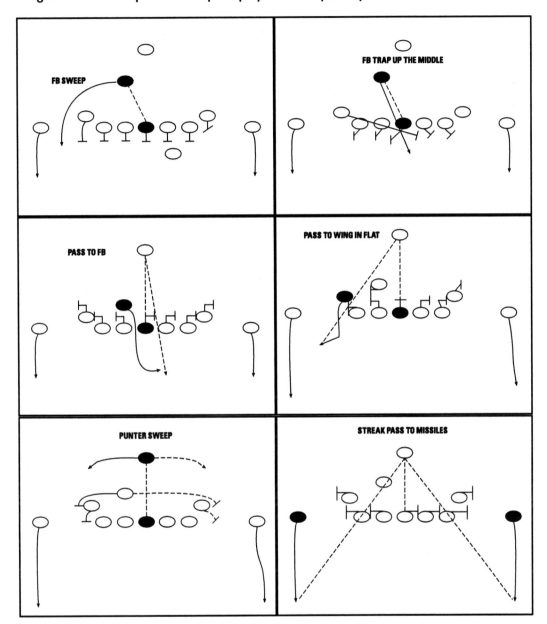

CHAPTER 6

KICKOFF COVER

For the sake of simplicity, the advice and information on kickoff cover that is presented in this chapter refers to college yard lines and hash marks. Thus, the high school coach will need to adjust any adopted schemes to high school yard lines and hash marks.

The primary goal for the kickoff cover unit is to keep the return inside the 25-yard line. In reference to the field position chart in chapter 1, the chances of the offense scoring when starting from inside the 25-yard line is quite poor. To meet this goal, the ball must be kicked deep, and the coverage players must sprint from the start, be aggressive and gang tackle.

Some teams will kick high bloopers and squibs to reduce the risk of long returns. While they may accomplish their goal of keeping the return yardage to a minimum, they will give up field position in the process. The real measure of a good kickoff cover team is the opponent's average start line, not their return average. On the other hand, some situations exist where such kicks are effective as change-ups.

COVERAGE PRINCIPLES

The following coverage principles apply to the kickoff cover team:

- Stance. The kickoff team members should face and look at the kicker. Their hips should be open slightly to the return team with their feet staggered slightly to facilitate a smooth crossover stride at the start.

- Starting procedure. After the referee has signaled the ball ready for play, the kicker should start his approach to the ball. When using BULLETS, the kicker will lower his raised hand to signal his BULLETS in motion and the start of his approach. The kickoff team members should time their approach to be at top speed when the ball is kicked. As the ball is kicked, and as the kickoff team members hit the line at top speed, they must see where the ball is kicked to adjust their coverage lanes.

- Coverage guidelines:

    ❑ It is imperative that everyone stays onsides. Everyone must stay behind the kicker. The kickoff team should hit the line as a unit at full speed.

    ❑ The unit's goal is to be aggressive, and gang tackle, and either cause a turnover or make the tackle inside their opponent's 20-yard line.

    ❑ The coverage must be an all-out sprint from the start. Everyone must at least cross the 30-yard line when the ball is caught.

    ❑ At the "contact point", the ball must be leveraged from the outside--in. Everyone should squeeze down the running lane with as much speed as possible, but under enough control to make the tackle.

    ❑ It is important that every member of the kickoff cover team stay in his coverage lane only as long as it takes to read the return. When an opponent attacks early, everyone must avoid him by releasing past him and working quickly back into their lane (weave technique). Each member of the kickoff unit should use his hands and push-off blockers that cross his face. If the ballcarrier is within 10 yards, everyone must stay in their lane and attack the blocker down the middle and use their hands to control him. Everyone must shed the blocker quickly and slide laterally to make the hit (two-gap technique), or shoot and run him into the returner if he is in a back peddle.

    ❑ Everyone must have the presence to feel where the ball is being returned. The direction or return indicator may help. This factor can provide everyone with a jump on adjusting their coverage lanes. Avoid the blockers and find the return lane.

    ❑ If someone gets blocked, he cannot stay blocked. The kickoff cover unit cannot trade one-for-one. Take out two!

    ❑ Never follow a teammate downfield. If a kickoff cover unit member comes off a release and sees a teammate crossing in front of him, he should work to the open lane (replace technique).

    ❑ The first man to the ball should take a controlled shot at the ballcarriers, attempting to: first, make the tackle; second, cause a fumble; and third, slow him by forcing him to change his course. This will give his teammates time to get there and clean up. The ball should be covered. Turnovers should be created.

❏ Tackle high with balance and control. Lock up and hang on. Gang tackling is simply a part of kickoff coverage.

❏ The kickoff is the best way to start convincing a team that they are going to be attacked from beginning to end.

❏ The reason a player is on the kickoff team is that he is one of the fastest, toughest men on the team. SPRINT AND GANG TACKLE!

❏ Get to the 20-yard line before the ballcarrier does. HUSTLE!

❏ Cover every kick—no one knows when a returner will bring it out of the end zone.

❏ Penetrate the front-five blockers. If three or more of the front five make their blocks, the return team has the advantage. If three or more cover men penetrate past the front five, the cover team has the advantage.

The chart in Table 6-1 illustrates the steps that the kickoff team should go through in covering the kickoff. It is important that players are drilled in the proper techniques and fundamentals required to perform all four of the steps outlined.

Table 6-1. The thought process in covering a kickoff.

CONTACT AND TACKLE	STEP #4	Determine the distance to the ball. Within 10 yards of ball: • Split the double-team • Two-gap the single blocker • Shoot and run a retreating blocker
Beat the blocker: • RUN PAST HIM • GET-ON-TOP • BEAT HIS TECHNIQUE **Avoid the front-five blockers**	STEP #3	• Manipulate the blocker, weave, and/or collision and backdoor. • Contact is not necessary.
Sprint and adjustment: • Flight of the ball • Safeties' path • Wedge setup ⟩ Return indicator • Frontline setup • Huddle call	STEP #2	• Keep your head downfield • Sprint at maximum speed • See and feel
Get off: • Stance • Proper vision • Accelerate	STEP #1	• Hit the restraining line at full speed • Be onsides

BASIC GUIDELINES FOR KICKOFF COVER UNIT MEMBERS

- *THE CALL:* First, gather on the sideline for any specific instruction. The "call" will be made in the huddle by the "call man", while the kicker is placing the ball. Possible calls (remind the team where the tee is placed, middle, left hash, or right hash):

   ❏ Deep (right, left, or middle)

   ❏ Squib (right, left, or middle)

   ❏ Bloop (right or left)

   ❏ Onside kick

   ❏ Overshift onside left or right

- *THE HUDDLE:* Huddle on the 25-yard line. After the break, move quickly to the specified alignment.

Diagram 6-1. An example of the kickoff cover team huddling for a middle kickoff.

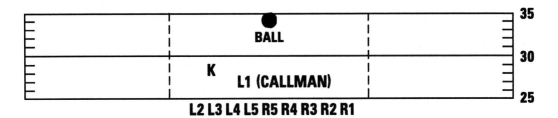

- *ALIGNMENT AND SPACING:*

   ❏ L1&R1—Align four yards from the sideline with the front foot on the 30-yard line.

   ❏ L2&R2—Align on bottom of the college numbers with the front foot on the 27-yard line.

   ❏ L3&R3—Align halfway between the adjacent #2 and the adjacent #4 with the back foot on the 25-yard line.

   ❏ L4&R4—Align on the hash with the front foot on the 25-yard line.

   ❏ L5&R5—Align on the post with the front foot on the 25-yard line.

- Bullet: Change the initial alignment from kick-to-kick. Never cross in front of the kicker while in motion and stay onsides.

- Kicker: Place the tee on either hash or in the middle of the field, depending on the call. Accuracy and hang time are critically important.

Diagram 6-2. Spacing and alignment of the kickoff cover team.

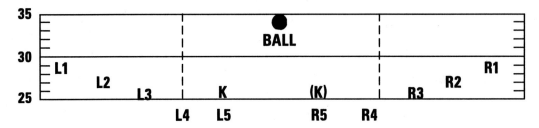

Note: The kickoff cover unit should always be alert for reverse or throwback returns. The 1's, 2's, 3's should never get outflanked by a wedge player or returner.

Diagram 6-3. Possible reverse and throwback returns.

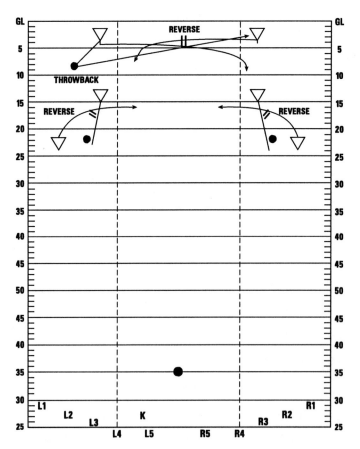

KICKOFF COVERAGE ASSIGNMENTS VS. A MIDDLE RETURN:

- *L1 & R1:* Secondary force (fold/bounce). Come to balance at 25-yard line. Keep #2 and the ball in front and inside of you (2x2 relationship). Never let the ball outside of you, force the ball out of bounds if the returner bounces to the sideline.

- *L2 & R2:* Force. Never let the ball outside you. Outside-tackle gap control (never allow two blockers outside you). Lane=tight outside tackle. Eyes=direct first to the tackle (frontline key), then to the end and near back, and finally to the backside returner (determine if he is setting up frontside or backside of the wedge). If wedge, attack the outside blocker in the wedge with your inside shoulder, keeping your outside arm free. If you go around the wedge, you must make the play.

- *L3 & R3:* Inside tackle gap control. Fill to the wedge.

- *L4 & R4:* Inside guard gap control. Fill to the wedge.

- *L5 & R5:* Center/guard gap control. Never get blocked by the center. Fill to the wedge.

Diagram 6-4. Kickoff coverage assignments against a middle return.

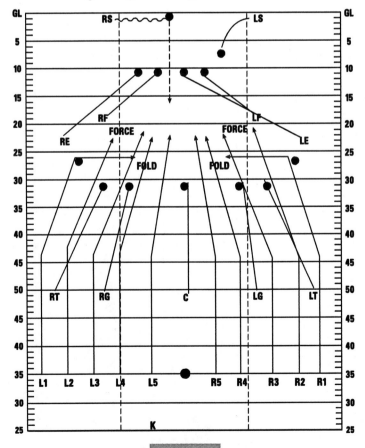

DEEP-LEFT KICKOFF—1's & 2's COVERAGE ASSIGNMENTS VS. BOUNDARY RETURN LEFT

RETURN SIDE

- #1: Secondary force (fold/bounce). Never let the ball outside you. Force the ball out of bounds if the returner bounces to the sideline. Lane—keep #2 in front and inside of you (2x2 relationship). Same with the ball—keep the ball in front and inside you.

- #2 Force. Never let the ball outside you. Outside – tackle gap control (never allow two blockers outside you). Lane—tight outside tackle. Eyes—direct first to the tackle (your frontline key), then to the end and near back, and finally to the backside returner (determine if he is setting up frontside or backside of the wedge). One/two gap in the wedge.

BACKSIDE

- #1: Read the end. Come to balance at the 25-yard line, fold/bounce. If the end goes away, slow-to-flow (safety).

- #2: Run at the tackle's outside shoulder, but stay outside the end. Stay outside the end who blocks you, but tight on his outside shoulder. Follow the end to the wedge (force). Can go under the backside returner without the ball.

Diagram 6-5.

Deep-left kickoff coverage assignments on a return left.

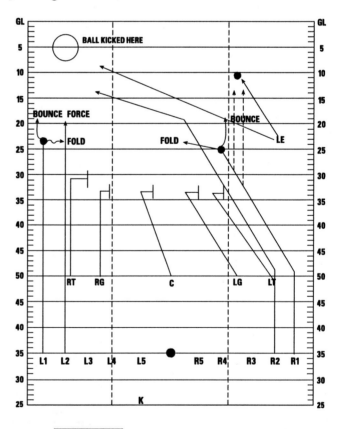

DEEP-LEFT KICKOFF—3's, 4's, and 5's COVERAGE ASSIGNMENTS VS. BOUNDARY RETURN LEFT

RETURN SIDE

- #3: Outside the tackle if he is blocking inside on #4 (get his hands on the tackle to help #4). Inside the tackle if he is blocking out on you. Attack the 2/3 gap in the wedge (split double team).

- #4: Release to the side of the return. Attack the 3/4 gap in the wedge (split the double-team).

- #5: Release to the side of the return. Two-gap #4 in wedge.

BACKSIDE

- #3: Inside the tackle and man/man on the backside end (go with the end). Scrape if the ball goes into the wedge. Bounce if the ball bounces to the wide field.

- #4: Release to the side of return. Scrape to the wedge.

- #5: Release to the side of return. Scrape to the wedge.

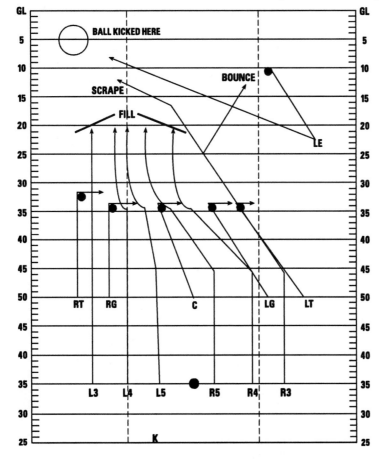

Diagram 6-6.

Deep-left kickoff coverage assignments for 3's, 4's, and 5's on a boundary return left.

DEEP-RIGHT KICKOFF—1's and 2's COVERAGE ASSIGNMENTS VS. BOUNDARY RETURN RIGHT

RETURN SIDE

- #1: Secondary Force (fold/bounce). Never let the ball outside you. Force the ball out of bounds if returner the bounces to the sideline. Lane—keep #2 in front and inside you. Same with the ball—keep the ball in front and inside you (2x2 relationship).

- #2: Force. Never let the ball outside you. Outside—tackle gap control (never allow two blockers outside you.) Lane—tight outside tackle. Eyes—direct first to the tackle (your frontline key), then to the end and near back, and finally to the backside returner (determine if he is setting up frontside or backside of the wedge). One/two gap in the wedge.

BACKSIDE

- #1: Read the end. Come to balance at the 25-yard line, fold/bounce. If the end goes away, slow-to-flow (safety).

- #2: Run at the tackle's outside shoulder, but stay outside the end. Stay outside the end who blocks you, but tight on his outside shoulder. Follow the end to the wedge (force). Can go under the backside returner without the ball.

Diagram 6-7.

Deep-right kickoff coverage assignments for 1's and 2's on a boundary return right.

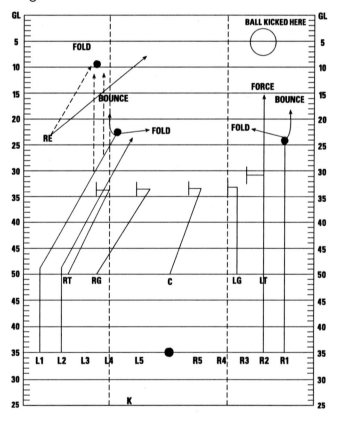

DEEP-RIGHT KICKOFF—3's, 4's, and 5's COVERAGE ASSIGNMENTS VS. BOUNDARY RETURN RIGHT

RETURN SIDE

- #3: Outside the tackle if he is blocking inside on #4 (get your hands on the tackle to help #4). Inside the tackle if he is blocking out on you. Attack the 2/3 gap in the wedge (split the double team).

- #4: Release to the side of the return. Attack the 3-4 gap in the wedge (split the double-team).

- #5: Release to the side of the return. Two-gap #4 in the wedge.

BACKSIDE

- #3: Inside the tackle and man/man on the backside end (go with the end). Scrape if the ball goes into the wedge. Bounce if the ball bounces to the wide field.

- #4: Release to the side of the return. Scrape to the wedge.

- #5: Release to the side of the return. Scrape to the wedge.

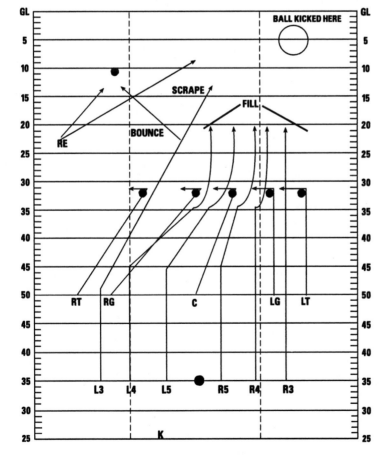

Diagram 6-8.

Deep-right kickoff coverage assignments on a boundary return left.

COVERAGE ASSIGNMENTS FOR ATTACKING THE WEDGE VS BOUNDARY RETURNS

Diagram 6-9. Boundary return left.

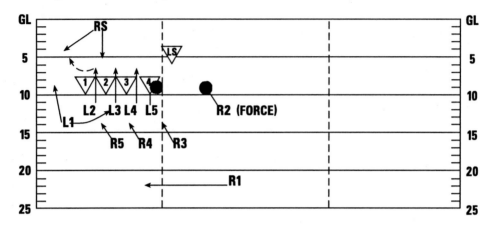

Diagram 6-10. Boundary return right.

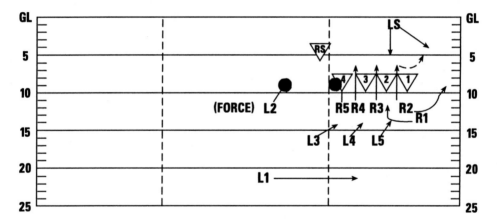

LEFT-HASH, BLOOP-RIGHT KICKOFF

NOTE: R1-L5 cheat their alignment to the right. L1-L4 Cheat their alignment to the right, but must be on the left side of the ball when it is kicked. Begin their "time-up" when the kicker lowers his arm.

Diagram 6-11. Left-hash, bloop-right kickoff.

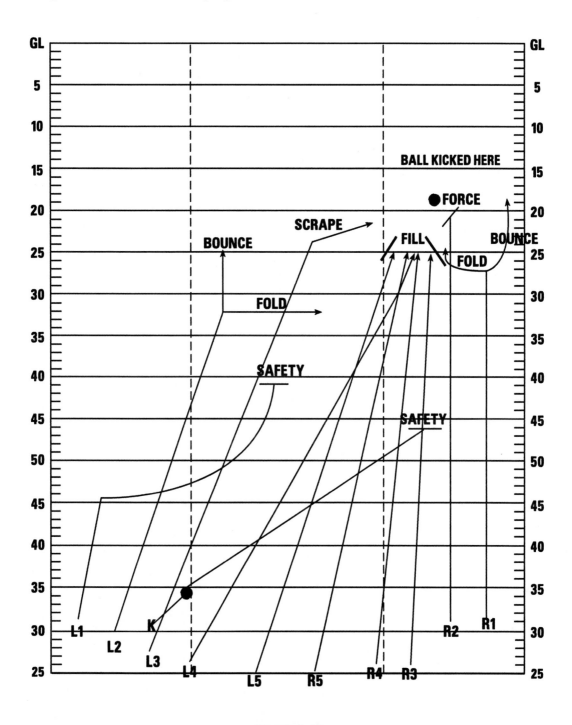

RIGHT-HASH, BLOOP-LEFT KICKOFF

NOTE: L1-R5 cheat their alignment to the left. R1-R4 cheat their alignment to the left, but must be on right side of the ball when it is kicked. The kickoff cover unit members should begin their "time-up" when the kicker lowers his arm.

Diagram 6-11. Right-hash, bloop-left kickoff.

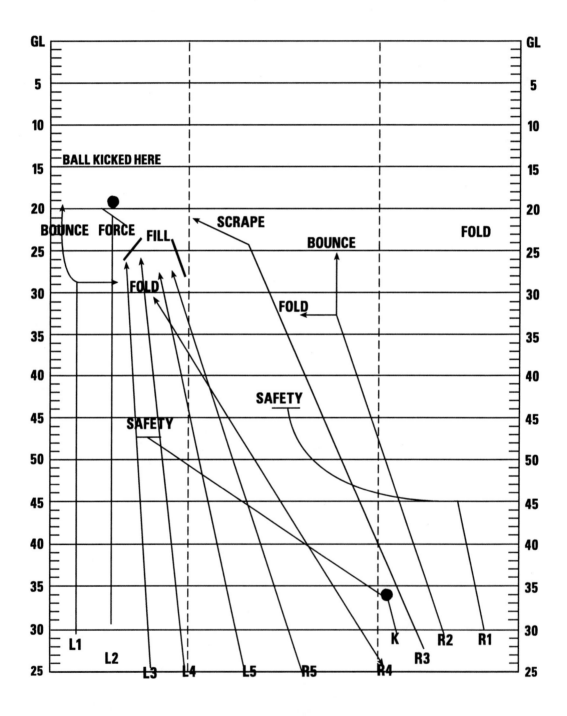

FREE KICK AFTER A SAFETY:

- The team against which a safety has been scored has the choice to punt or kick. (They will probably kick).

- The restraining line is the 20-yard line.

- The kick or punt will normally be made from the middle of the field.

- The kicking team will align in your normal kickoff alignment. However, the restraining line is the 20-yard line.

- Remember—a punter's approach will be different than a kicker's approach.

- All kickoff rules apply, regardless of whether a team punts or kicks.

Diagram 6-13. Free kick after a safety.

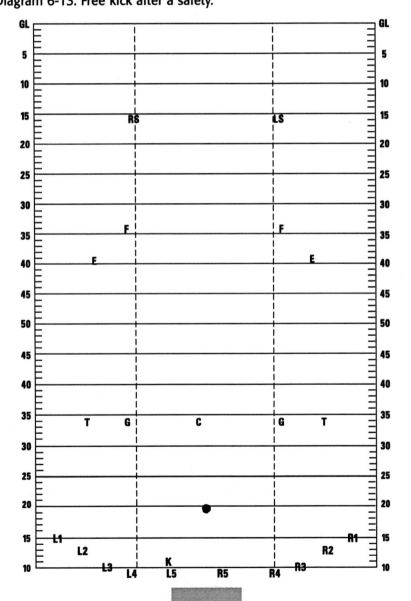

RIGHT-HASH, ONSIDE-KICK LEFT

GENERAL INFORMATION:

At least four players must be on each side of the ball when it is kicked. The alignment of L1-L5 and R5 should be cheated to the left. The kickoff cover team should also align on the 30-yard line instead of the 25-yard line. They should DISGUISE THEIR STRATEGY! They should keep in mind that the ball is theirs after it has traveled 10 yards.

ASSIGNMENTS:

L1 – Keep the ball on the field. Recover it before it goes out of bounds.

L2 – Shield the tackle. If the ball crosses his face, recover it.

L3 & L4 – Follow the ball and recover it after 10 yards.

L5 – Shield the guard. If the ball crosses his face, recover it.

R5 – Shield the center. If the ball crosses his face, recover it.

R4 – He is a short safety 10-12 yards from the ball. Protect vs. a return.

R3 – He is the deep safety, twenty yards from the ball. Center up and mirror the football.

R2 – He is force; protect vs. any return. Keep outside leverage on the football.

R1 – He is a short safety, 10-12 yards from the ball. Protect vs. a return.

Kicker – The game plan dictates the type of kick. Follow the kick; be alert to recover a muff.

Diagram 6-14. Right-hash, onside-kick left.

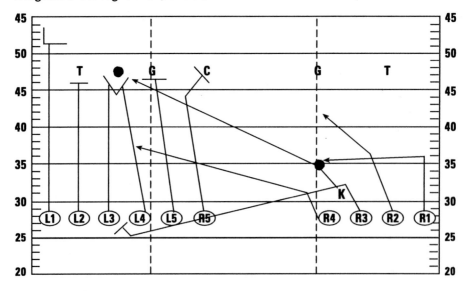

LEFT-HASH, ONSIDE-KICK RIGHT

GENERAL INFORMATION:

At least four players must be on either side of the ball when it is kicked. The alignment of R1-R5 and L5 should be cheated to the right. The kickoff cover unit should also align on the 30-yard line instead of the 25-yard line. They should DISGUISE THEIR STRATEGY! They should keep in mind that the ball is theirs after it has traveled 10 yards.

ASSIGNMENTS:

R1 – Keep the ball on the field. Recover it before it goes out of bounds.

R2 – Shield the tackle. If the ball crosses his face, recover it.

R3 & R4 – Follow the ball and recover it after 10 yards.

R5 – Shield the guard. If the ball crosses his face, recover it.

L5 – Shield the center. If the ball crosses his face, recover it.

L4 – He is a short safety 10-12 yards from the ball. Protect vs. a return.

L3 – He is the deep safety, twenty yards from the ball. Center up and mirror the football.

Kicker – The game plan dictates the type of kick. Follow the kick; be alert to recover a muff.

Diagram 6-15. Left-hash, onside-kick right.

CHAPTER 7

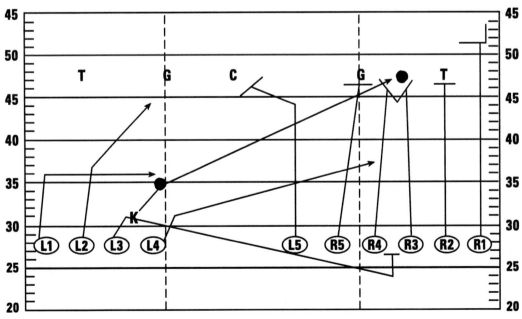

KICKOFF RETURN

Similar to the previous chapter, (again, for the sake of simplicity), the information presented in this chapter on kickoff returns uses refer to college yard lines and hash marks as reference points. Thus, high school coaches need to adjust any adopted schemes to high school yard lines and hash marks.

The primary goal for the kickoff return unit is to gain possession of the ball in good field position when the play is over. This sounds simplistic; however, it takes a complex set of successfully executed assignments to accomplish this objective. Not surprisingly, the kickoff return team must stay free of penalties to accomplish their goal.

Ideally, the kickoff return is designed to score. In reality, this is very difficult to do. On the other hand, even just returning the ball to good field position helps the offense begin their series with a lot of options, and eliminates the stress about punching it out from inside the 20-yard line.

KICKOFF RETURN PRINCIPLES:

The following guidelines apply to kickoff returns:

- Field all kicks. It is a free ball after going 10 yards. Down it or return it, unless you are sure it is going out of bounds.

- Always see the ball kicked. Know the direction of the kick so that every one can set their wedges and blocks properly.

- Block in front and above the waist. Clipping or an illegal block in the back can cost the team 50 yards or six points. Your team can end up back on its own 10-yard line rather than at mid-field. It is not worth it. Hold off if you cannot block an opponent legally. Play smart!

- Be prepared and determined you are going to successfully carry out your assignment. Get your man. Study him on film. Football is often a game of inches.

- Second effort means you get up off the ground after throwing your first block. Go block someone else. Chase the ball carrier.

- After the kick, keep your eyes on your man. Block him at the right time. Timing is important.

- The wedge blockers must have the toughness to run through people.

- The front-five blockers must be able to "contact-fit" and stay with their block.

- The members of the kickoff return unit may fair catch a kickoff. Example—a high blooper into a strong wind (usually fielded by the wedge people).

- Always anticipate an "onside kick" if the kick return unit has incurred a 15-yard penalty that allows the other team to kickoff from mid-field.

- Be alert for a squib kickoff if the opponent is kicking into a strong wind.

- On directional returns (left or right), the kickoff return team should "convert" only when the ball is kicked short to the safety who is opposite the callside.

POSITION NOTES: (KICKOFF RETURN)

FRONT FIVE (GUARDS, TACKLES AND CENTER):

- Never line up directly in front of the ball. Always offset to avoid a hard kick directly at you.

- Always expect either the hard kick at you, or an onside kick first. Fall on the onside kick. Let the hard kick go on by you.

- Know your blocking assignment. Communicate with your teammates.

- Align behind the 45-yard line (i.e., the front restraining line) until the ball is kicked. The front-5 blockers usually align with their back foot on the 48-yard line.

- After you see the ball kicked deep, turn and sprint back to your blocking point. Find your man. It is imperative that you see the direction and distance of the kick.

- Make your blocks at least 5-10 yards in front of the wedge.

- Listen and look for calls as to adjust your blocking angle.

- The center is responsible to notice directional kicks by the laces on the ball, and/or the position of the kicker.

- Whe the center yells, "squib" or "bloop", the front five should short set on the 40-yard line.

WEDGE PLAYERS: (A, B, C, D'S):

- Must always be alert for line-drive kicks, bloop kicks, squib kicks and onside kicks.

- "C or B" should set the wedge on the catch and also make the calls (squib, short, etc.).

- Wedge players should be a good blocker, runner and ballhandler.

- Only one player is responsible to "set" the wedge. The others should set on him.

- Listen for calls to adjust your blocking responsibility.

- See where the ball is kicked (during flight) in order to locate the wedge.

- A, B, C, and D should never back up to catch a kick; they should catch only balls kicked in front of them when the safety doesn't call for it.

SAFETIES (RETURNERS):

One safety is the designated "return safety". The other safety should handle only a small percentage of kicks. Both players must be familiar with the following:

- Practice sound fundamentals when handling the ball. Look the ball into your hands. Tuck it away tight (four points of pressure). Get in the habit of keeping a tight grip on the nose of the ball with your fingers and hands. Put pressure on the rear of the ball with your elbow and arm. Learn to run with the ball in a secure position. You can let the ball swing back and forth in a natural rhythm and still keep the ball in close to your body, with the pressure tightly applied front and rear. When you get trapped, bring the ball in close and protect it with both hands. If you think about these good fundamentals and do them in practice, it will be automatic in a game.

- Handle all kickoffs (unless they're "short" kicks which the wedge will handle). Any muffed kickoff into the end zone must be covered and downed. If your opponent recovers the ball in the end zone, it is a touchdown for the other team.

- If you bring a ball out of the end zone, continue to return it upfield. Going back into the end zone would give your opponent a safety (either if you down it, or if they tackle you).

- A cool head is required in your job. Always be thinking!

- A bouncing kickoff that ricochets off you or one of your teammates into the end zone can be downed there for a touchback, and you get the ball on our 20-yard line. (The impetus that sent the kick into the end zone came from the kicker, even though it may have bounced off you, or one of your teammates.)

- Watch the kicker's angle to anticipate a corner kick. Also, notice where the strings of the ball are pointing. Be thinking what to do if the kickoff goes into a corner of the field. The center will help you by raising his hand to the side of the kick.

- Catching a kick going forward is one basic fundamental of achieving good returns. Because the kicking team knows also this, they frequently try to prevent this from happening by kicking the ball to the corner. If they can get you to field the ball going sideways or backwards, your momentum will be slowed effectively.

- Another tactic to nullify a good return man is to SQUIB kick. Field these types of balls as quickly as possible and get all you can.

- A kick that goes 3, 4, or 5 yards deep into the end zone requires good judgment as to whether or not you should run it out. The scouting report will be especially important in this instance. TALK TO EACH OTHER! The height of the kick should help you make your decision. Also know what yard line the ball has been kicked from.

- Know the kicker (e. g., where he puts the ball, average distance, height and hang time, etc.).

- Be conscious of the wind—is the ball being kicked with it or against it? How strong is the wind?

- Talk to each other to be sure who is catching the ball. The "right safety" should give a loud and clear, "you..you..you" or "me..me..me" call. He should pound his chest with his right hand on, "me..me", and point with his left hand on, "you..you."

- Know the coverage—how the kickoff team comes down the field, and any habits they may have.

- Be "reckless runners"—SCORE!

    - ❑ BE SMART!

    - ❑ EXERT AT HIGH VELOCITY!

    - ❑ FINISH!

COMMUNICATION

Proper communication among the returners and between the returners and wedge is critical in handling the ball and avoiding mishaps. The "kickoff communication" chart illustrated in Diagram 7-1 provides one example of how to properly communicate who should handle the ball.

Diagram 7-1. A sample kickoff communication chart.

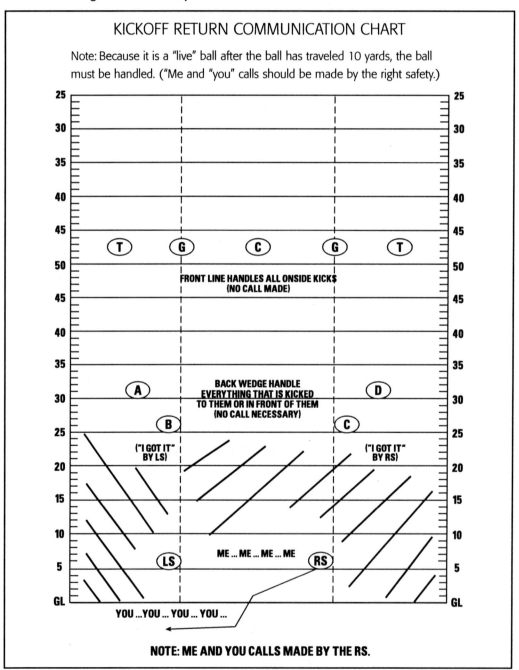

KICKOFF RETURN THOUGHT PROCESS FOR THE FRONT FIVE
AND THE WEDGE

FRONT FIVE: The process covers from the 45-yard line to approximately the opposite 30-yard line. Short set on the 40-yard line vs. bloop or squib kicks.

Diagram 7-2. Kickoff return thought process for the front five.

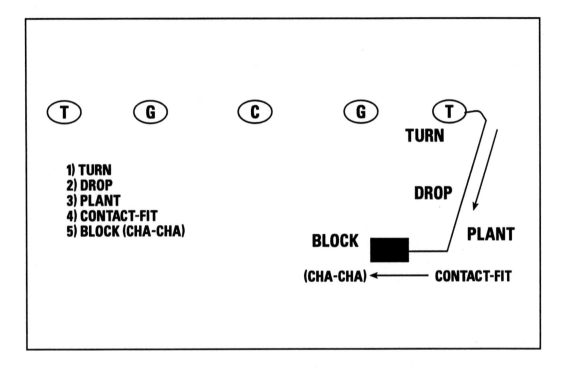

WEDGE: The process covers from the 25-yard line to the 10-yard line (approximately 15 yards) depending on the following guidelines involving wedge mechanics:

- All wedge personnel must see the ball kicked and always be alert for line-drive kicks, bloop kicks, squib kicks and onside kicks.

- See where the ball is kicked in order to be better prepared so as to anticipate the location of the wedge.

- "B" should set the wedge on the catch by LS. "C" should set the wedge on the catch by RS. All others should set on him.

- "C" or "B" should set the wedge 8-10 yards in front of the ball, but not any wider than the numbers. Yell, "GO-GO" on the catch to get the wedge moving. On veer right or left, direct the path of the wedge toward the tackle to the veer side.

- All wedge personnel should eyeball the kick for direction and then locate "B" or "C". Establish a position shoulder-to-shoulder with the next man inside them. Settle and face upfield with their shoulders square. Stagger their feet and be ready to take off on the "GO-GO" command, toward the tackle to the veer side.

- The safety not catching the ball should follow the call safety's, "me" or "you" call. Make sure the ball is securely caught, and then join the edge of the wedge on his side. Block the edger to his side.

- The safety catching the ball should follow the call safety's, "me" or "you" call. After making the catch, start straight upfield behind the wedge and veer with them; look for a seam and hit it full speed. SCORE!

- The wedge should not be set wider than the numbers on the field.

Diagram 7-3. Wedge mechanics.

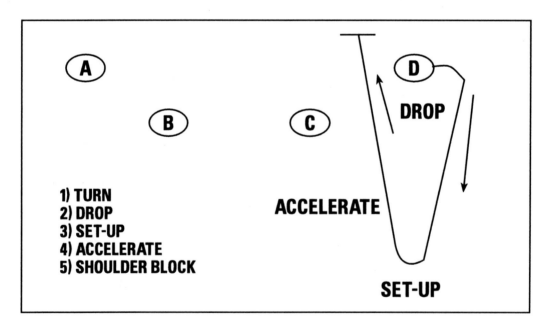

EXAMPLES OF VARIOUS KICKOFF RETURNS

Table 7-1. Assignments for a right return with a double-team block.

POSITION	ALIGNMENT	ASSIGNMENT	TECHNIQUE
LEFT TACKLE:	Front foot on the +47-yard line. Split the difference between the hash and sideline.	Block #8—out.	Reverse drop to 30-yard line (can drop deeper if necessary). Block #8 away from the running lane.
LEFT GUARD:	Front foot on the +47-yard line. Just inside the left hash.	Block #7—out.	Reverse drop to 30-yard line. Block #7 away from running lane.
CENTER:	Front foot on the +47-yard line in the middle of the field (offset the ball if it is placed in middle of field).	Block #6—out.	Drop to the 30-yard line. Block #6 away from running lane.
RIGHT GUARD:	Front foot on the +47-yard line, just inside of right hash.	Block #5—in.	Drop to the 30-yard line. Block #5 away from the running lane.
RIGHT TACKLE:	Front foot on the +47-yard line. Split the difference between the hash marks and the sideline.	Block #4—in.	Drop to the 30-yard line. Block #4 away from the running lane.
A	On the 25-yard line. Split the difference between the left guard and left tackle.	Double-team #4 with the RT.	Drop to wedge (eight yards in front of the safety). Straight line to #4. Don't chase him. If he goes outside the, double-team #5 or keep going to the safety.
B	On the 20-yard line, just inside of the left guard.	Block #3.	Set the wedge eight yards in front of the catch. Block #3.
C (wedge setter)	On the 20-yard line, just inside of the right guard.	Block #1 or #2—out.	Drop to wedge (eight yards in front of the safety). Kick out #1 or #2. Yell, "go" after the catch.
D	On the 25-yard line. Split the difference between the right guard and the right tackle.	Block #1 or #2—out.	Drop to the wedge (eight yards in front of the safety). Kick out #1 or #2.
LEFT SAFETY	On the 5-yard line, just inside of the left hash, depending on the kicker's abilities, tendencies, wind, and tee.	Block the edger. If no edger, double-team #5 with the RG.	See the ball caught by the safety. Get into the wedge. Block the edger. If no edger, straight-line to #5 and the DT with #5. Don't chase him.
RIGHT SAFETY	On the 5-yard line, just inside of the right hash, depending on the kicker's abilities, tendencies, wind, and tee.	Field ball.	The running lane is between D, C, and B, or cut-back to DT on #4. SCORE!!

Relative to the blocking assignments outlined in Table 7-1, it should be noted that the kickoff return unit has the option of zoning the wedge, rather than blocking an assigned number. This option is determined by the game plan. In addition, the left tackle may be required to reroute #8 and peel to the running lane. On a blooper or squib kick, the front five should short set on the 40-yard line.

Diagram 7-4. A right return with a double-team on #4 with the RT and A.

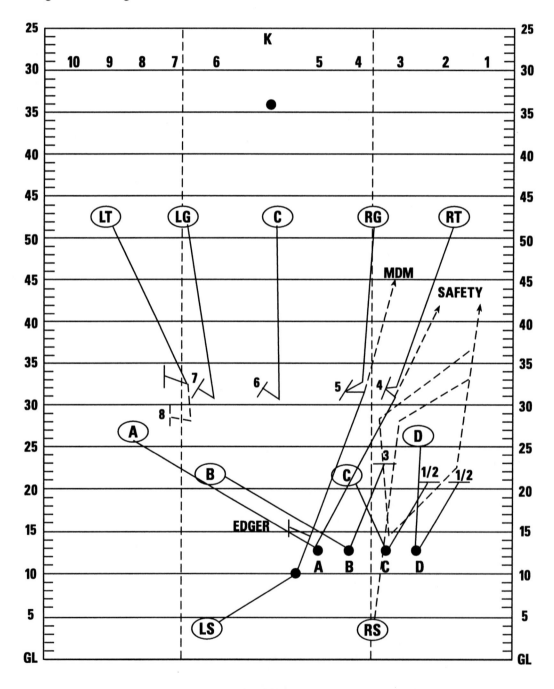

Diagram 7-5. A right return with a double-team on #4 by the RG and RT.

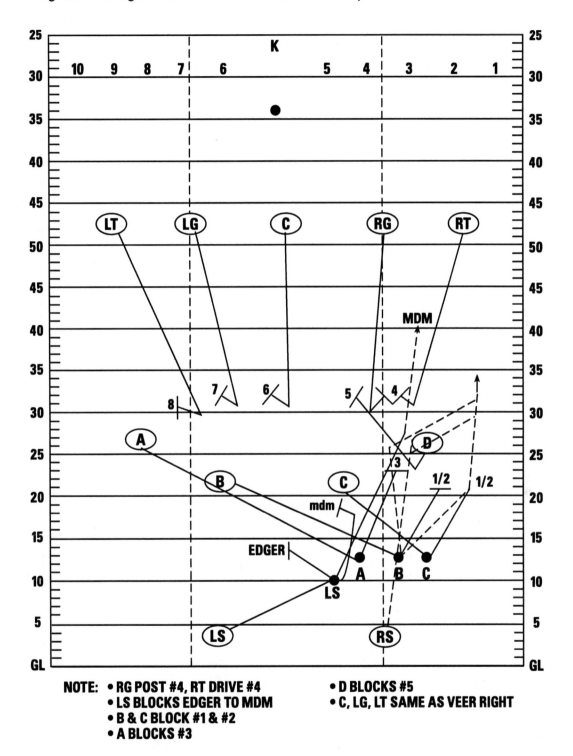

NOTE: • RG POST #4, RT DRIVE #4   • D BLOCKS #5
      • LS BLOCKS EDGER TO MDM   • C, LG, LT SAME AS VEER RIGHT
      • B & C BLOCK #1 & #2
      • A BLOCKS #3

Diagram 7-6. A left return with a double-team on #8 by LT and C.

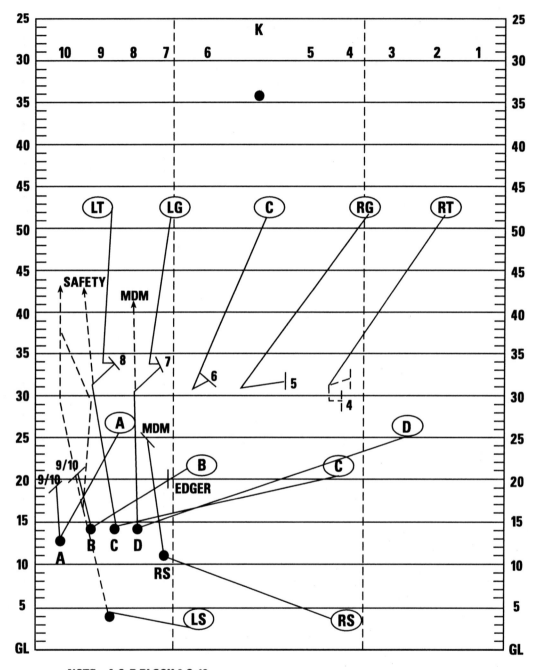

NOTE: A & B BLOCK 9 & 10
C: STRAIGHT LINE TO #8 & DOUBLE TEAM WITH LT. DON'T CHASE HIM.
    IF HE GOES OUTSIDE, DOUBLE TEAM #7 OR KEEP GOING TO SAFETY.
D: STRAIGHT LINE TO #7 & DOUBLE TEAM WITH LG.
    DON'T CHASE HIM, KEEP GOING TO MDM.

Diagram 7-7. A veer-left return with C and D blocking the MDM.

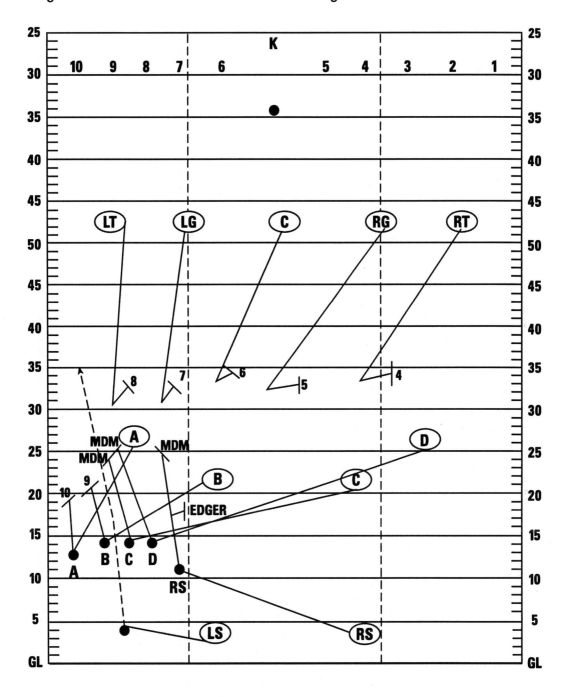

Diagram 7-8. A counter-left return.

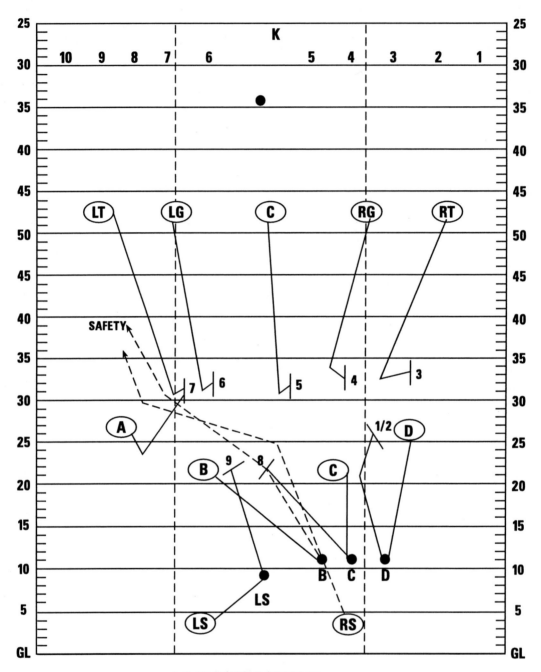

A & LT DOUBLE TEAM #7
LS, B & C BLOCK OUT ON #8 & #9
D-BLOCK #1 OR #2 (THE EDGER)

Table 7-2. Assignments for a counter-left return with a double-team block.

POSITION	ALIGNMENT	ASSIGNMENT	TECHNIQUE
LEFT TACKLE	Front foot on the +47-yard line. Split the difference between the hash marks and the sideline.	Block #7—in.	Drop to the 30-yard line. Look at #8 and block #7—in. *Double-Team with A.
LEFT GUARD	Front foot on the +47-yard line near the hash mark.	Block #6—in.	*Drop to 30-yard line. Look at #7 and block #6—in.
CENTER	Front foot on the +47-yard line in the middle of the field (offset the ball if it is placed in middle of field).	Block #5—out.	*Drop to the 30-yard line. Look at #6 and block #5—out.
RIGHT GUARD	Front foot on the +47-yard line near the hash mark.	Block #4—out.	*Drop to the 30-yard line. Look at #5 and block #4—out.
RIGHT TACKLE	Front foot on the +47-yard line. Split the difference between the hash marks and the sideline.	Block #3—out.	Drop to the 30-yard line. Look at #4 and block #3—out.
A	On the 25-yard line, split the difference between the left guard and left tackle.	Double-team #7 with LT.	*Double-team #7 with LT. Stay on LT's right shoulder.
B	On the 20-yard line, just inside of the left guard.	Double-team #8 with C.	*Drop to the wedge. Double-team #8—out with C.
C (WEDGESETTER)	On the 20-yard line, just inside of the right guard. (Five-yard offset to left of RS.)	Double-team #8 with B.	*Set the wedge. Straight line to #8 with B. If B blocks #8, keep going to the safety.
D	On the 25-yard line, split the difference between the right guard and right tackle.	Block #1 or #2—out.	*Drop to the wedge. Block #1 or #2—out. (Edger.).
LEFT SAFETY	On the 5-yard line. The width depends on the kick spot. The depth depends on the kicker's ability, wind, tendencies.	Block #9 or MDM.	Set up on the hip of B. Block #9 out or MDM.
RIGHT SAFETY	On the 5-yard line, the width depends on the kick spot. The depth depends on the kicker's ability, wind, tendencies.	Field the ball.	Take the ball upfield, and then veer to the wideside and find a running lane off B and C's double team. SCORE!

With regard to the assignments outlined in Table 7-2, it should be noted that the wedge blockers' assignments can be changed up, depending on the opponent's coverage responsibilities. On a squib kick, the front 5 should short set on the 40-yard line.

Diagram 7-9. A counter-right return.

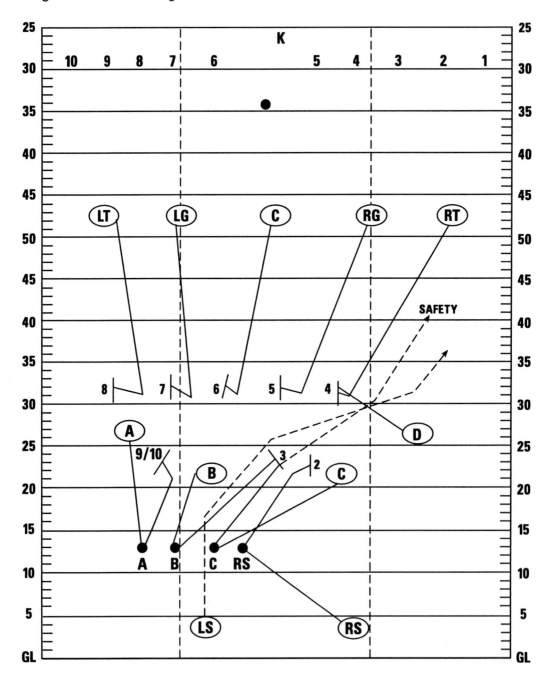

Table 7-3. Assignments for a counter-right return with a double-team block.

POSITION	ALIGNMENT	ASSIGNMENT	TECHNIQUE
LEFT TACKLE	Front foot on the +47-yard line. Split the difference between the hash marks and sideline.	Block #8—out.	*Drop to the 30-yard line. Look at #7 and block #8—out.
LEFT GUARD	Front foot on the +47-yard line near the hash mark.	Block #7—out.	*Drop to the 30-yard line. Look at #6 and block #7—out.
CENTER	Front foot on the +47-yard line in the middle of the field (offset the ball if it is placed in the middle of the field).	Block #6—out.	*Drop to the 30-yard line. Look at #5 and block #6—out.
RIGHT GUARD	Front foot on the +47-yard line near the hash mark.	Block #5—in..	*Drop to the 30-yard. Look at #4 and block #5—in.
RIGHT TACKLE	Front foot on the +47-yard. Split the difference between the hash marks and the sideline.	Block #4—in.	Drop to the 30-yard line. Look at #3 and block #4—in. *Double-team with D.
A	On the 25-yard line, split the difference between the left guard and left tackle.	Block #9 or #10—out.	*Drop to the wedge; block #9 or #10—out. (Edger.).
B (WEDGE SETTER)	On the 20-yard line, just inside of the left guard. Five-yard offset to right of LS.	Double-team #3 with C.	*Set the wedge. Straight line to #3 and double-team #3 with C. If C blocks #3, keep going to the safety.
C	On the 20-yard line, just inside of the right guard.	Double-team #3 with B.	*Drop to wedge. Double-team #3 with B.
D	On the 25-yard line, split the difference between the right guard and right tackle.	Double #4 with RT.	*Double-team #3 with RT. Stay on the RT's left shoulder.
LEFT SAFETY	On the 5-yard line. The width depends on kick the spot. The depth depends on the kicker's ability, wind, tendencies.	Field the ball.	Take the ball upfield, and then veer to the wideside and find a running land off C and B's double-team. SCORE!
RIGHT SAFETY	On 5-yard line. The width depends on the kick spot. The depth depends on the kicker's ability, wind, tendencies.	Block #2.	Set up on the hip of C. Block #2 out or MDM.

With regard to the assignment outlined in Table 7-3, the wedge blockers' assignments can be changed up, depending on the opponent's coverage responsibilities. On a squib kick, the front 5 should short set on the 40-yard line.

Diagram 7-10. A middle-return (match-up).

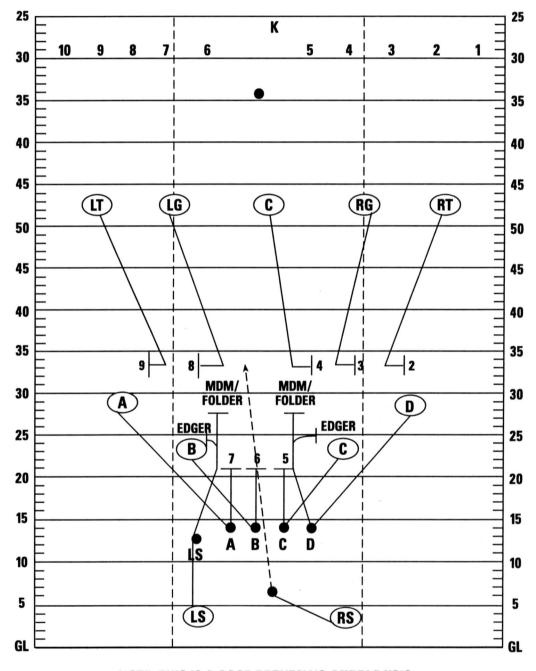

NOTE: THIS IS A GOOD RETURN VS. MIDDLE KO'S

DEFINITE ONSIDE KICK RETURN ("HANDS" TEAM)

HANDS TEAM PERSONNEL:

Special personnel should be substituted for the normal kickoff return personnel when anticipating an onside kick. These players should possess both great hands for fielding the ball and quick reactions to make split-second decisions.

ALIGNMENT:

- Center – Middle of the field (on the +46-yard line), offset the ball.
- Guards – On or near the hashmarks (on the +46-yard line).
- Tackles – Split the difference between the hash and sideline (on the +46-yard line). The tackles should never get outflanked by the widest coverage man.
- A, B, C, D – Align in the gaps (49-yard line); they must be able to see the ball in their stance. Be alert for overshift.
- Safeties – On the hashmarks (on the 25-yard line).

ONSIDE KICK PRINCIPLES:

- Stay square to the football in a good fundamental football position with your hands positioned as a baseball infielder.
- Field any onside attempt directly at you or close to the restraining line. Fielding a kick that is close to the line requires good judgment. Field it if there is any doubt as to whether it is going to cross the line, and you can recover it clearly (i.e., on the big hop).
- If the kick goes through the front line, the front people will block in front of the kick; A, B, C, D will recover. Fall on the ball.
- A loose ball close to the sidelines must be batted-out-of-bounds.
- Remember you may "fair catch" short bloop kicks.
- If the opponent kicks deep, block the man aligned in front of you.
- Safeties – Field all kicks in front and behind you in the field of play and return them when you can. Protect the ball. If the ball is kicked in the end zone, down it.!! Remember, you may "fair catch" short kicks!

Diagram 7-11. Hands team alignment when the ball is in the middle of the field.

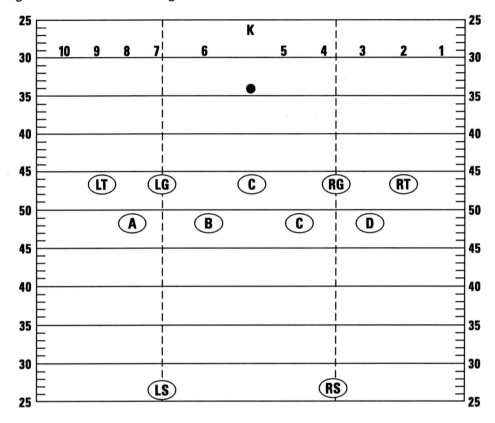

HANDS TEAM ADJUSTMENTS:

Diagram 7-12. Shift right adjustment by the hands team to motion right.

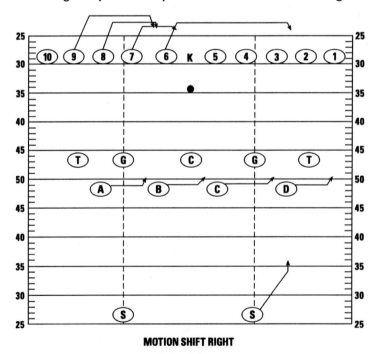

MOTION SHIFT RIGHT

Diagram 7-13. Shift left adjustment by the hands team to motion left.

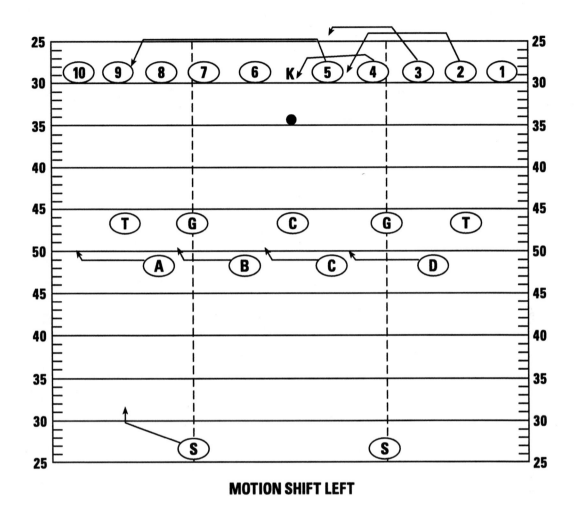

MOTION SHIFT LEFT

KICKOFF RETURN AFTER A SAFETY (EXECUTE THE CALLED RETURN)

Diagram 7-14. An example of a kickoff return after a safety.

CHAPTER 8

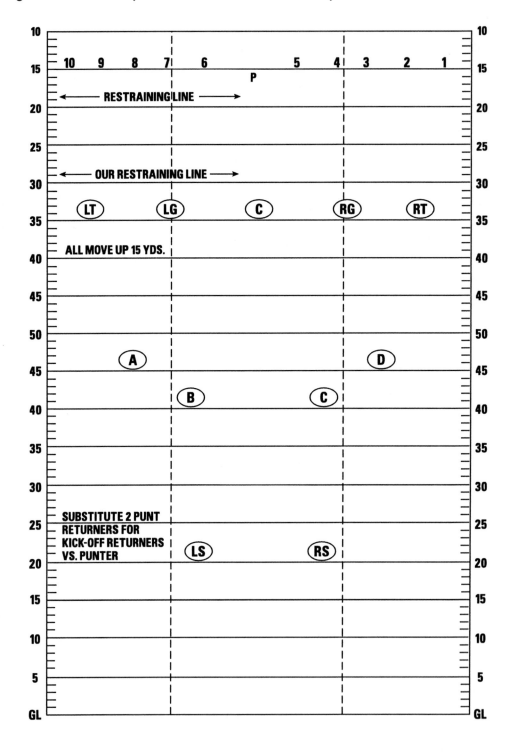

PAT/FG. AND PAT/FG DEFENSE

The PAT and FG

A point after touchdown or a field goal can never be a routine play. One team is trying to score; the other is trying to prevent the score. The point to keep in mind is: "Take the play off and you will get beat!" On these plays, effort and technique are critical, just like any offensive or defensive play.

In a typical season, about 30 percent of a team's total points scored are scored by the kicking units, and, almost all of these points are scored by the PAT/FG team. In this regard, the team goals should be:

- 100% PAT accuracy

- 100% FG accuracy inside the 40-yard line (kick spot)

The get off time (snap-to-kick) for the PAT/FG should be 1.3 seconds or less. Any slower than this increases the risk of getting the kick blocked.

Two different procedures are reviewed in this discussion of PAT/FG. First, the "swinging gate" for the PAT play. Second, a FG procedure that is different than the swinging gate. If the coach decides not to implement the swinging gate, the same procedures can be used for both the PAT and FG.

In order to execute the swinging gate at an optimum level of efficiency, extra meeting and practice time are required. On the other hand, utilizing the swinging gate also forces the opponent to spend extra practice time during the week preparing their team for all the variables presented by its use. These variables include the many possible fakes that can be run from the swinging gate, and the fakes that can be run after shifting into a normal kicking alignment.

P.A.T.

NO HUDDLE (SWINGING GATE):

- DO NOT HUDDLE in the one-point P.A.T. situation.

- All personnel should assume the swinging-gate formation as quickly as possible and listen for the call from the holder.

STANCE AND ALIGNMENT:

- LINEMEN (G's, T's, E's and snapper). The snapper must align first with his feet parallel and his inside foot on the left hashmark, facing the goal line with his hands on his knees and his heels on the 4-yard line. All other linemen should align in a toe-to-toe relationship with the snapper, facing the goal line with his hands on his knees and with a 4-6-inch split.

- WINGBACKS. The RW aligns on the 7-yard line, directly behind the snapper facing the ball. The LW aligns two yards behind the LOS with his inside foot behind the LW's outside foot. The LW faces the goal line with his hands on his knees.

- HOLDER. The holder aligns seven yards behind the ball (10-yard line), facing the goal line in upright position to read the defense's alignment.

- The kicker aligns at his normal kicking spot (i.e., 7.5 yards from the LOS). NOTE: All players must get aligned quickly and not move, since the holder may call a fake.

Diagram 8-1. Alignment for the swinging gate.

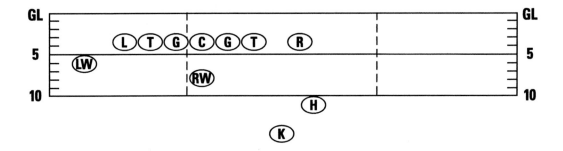

Diagram 8-2. Stance for the swinging gate.

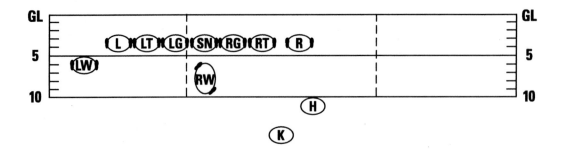

THE CALL (one of three calls will be made):

- Kick it

- Be alert to a possible fake (this is an either fake or a kick call)

- Execute the fake called

FIELD GOAL

HUDDLE:

- The unit will huddle, unless they have no time-outs and a "scramble" call is given. The field goal unit should huddle to the side nearest its bench, unless the ball is on the near hash; then the center should huddle the field goal team up at midfield (seven yards from LOS).

- Huddle call by the holder: "Field goal on the snap. Alert for FIRE! Ready, break."

Diagram 8-3.

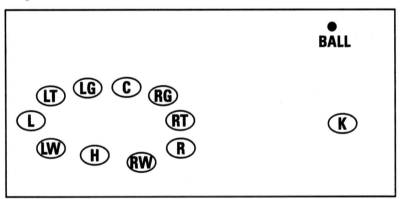

STANCE AND ALIGNMENT:

- LINEMEN (guards, tackles, ends). The linemen are aligned in a three-point, shoulder-width stance, with their outside foot staggered forward (toe-to-instep). Their inside foot should be placed outside of the next man's outside foot (i.e., their toe should be parallel with his heel). This positioning will allow them to step laterally inside to interlock legs. It is imperative that they see the football in their stance. The guards should interlock with the feet of the center on alignment before the snap.

- WINGBACKS. The wingbacks are in a fundamental football position with their hands on their knees, facing out at a 45-degree angle with their inside foot directly behind the tight end's butt, and a good two-feet deeper than his heels (double-bump technique).

- HOLDER. The holder's toe should be placed seven-and-one half yards behind the LOS.

Diagram 8-4.

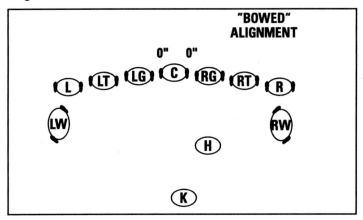

THE CALL:

- The holder should first look to see that the team is ready. Next, he should check to see that the kicker is ready. Next, he should call, "SET." The center then snaps the ball, following a one-second pause after "SET."

- No movement can occur after the "SET" command.

- Everyone should be alert for a "FIRE" call.

- If the QB is the holder, any fake call can be sent in with him.

ASSIGNMENTS AND BLOCKING TECHNIQUE:

- CENTER. After the set command, the center can snap the ball any time he is ready. The snap must be sharp and accurate. Smooth rhythm must exist with the snap, hold and kick. The center should use head movements to prevent the rush from getting a jump on the snap. After the snap, he should then set and raise up under control. He cannot fire out or get pulled—this would create a rush lane. He should be alert to cover on long field-goal attempts.

- GUARDS AND TACKLES. The guards and tackles should set low and tough and raise high and tight to the inside-block area. Initially, they should take a quick set step with their inside foot, sharply planting it just inside and behind the heel of the outside foot of the player inside of them. The should keep their outside foot planted and stationary and their shoulders and hips square to the LOS. They should also keep their hands high to block, as in pass protection. They should remember that they are responsible for the *inside gap first*. Be alert to cover on long field-goal attempts.

- ENDS AND WINGBACKS. They are responsible for the inside gap first, then their outside gap. Their first step should be to the inside to secure that gap. When using a "double-bump" technique, they should strike the inside rusher with their inside hand as they step inside, and then drop their outside foot back at a 45-degree angle and strike the outside rusher with their outside hand. The wings should always "peel back" and spy for a blocked kick. If a kick is blocked, they should recover the ball or make the tackle.

- HOLDER. He is as much responsible for a successful kick as the kicker. (Note: he is also responsible for ensuring that there are 11 men on the field.) Smooth rhythm must exist between the snap, hold and kick. The holder should place his down hand on the spot where he'll set the football. He should then check to see that the team and the kicker are ready. He should be alert to yell, "FIRE" on any malfunction. He is the right safety in coverages involving long field-goal attempts. On these attempts, he should make sure the spot has been properly placed at 7 ½ yards.

- KICKER. He should pick his spot for lining-up directly behind the ball. He may offset if the ball is on the hash. He should let the holder know when he is ready. Concentrating on the spot, he should begin his approach when the ball is snapped. (The holder's hand will tell him when to begin his approach). Normal rhythm is 1.3 seconds. He is the left safety in fieldgoal coverage. He should be alert to yell, "FIRE", on any malfunction.

FG ALIGNMENT VARIATIONS

"TACKLE OVER" CALL:

- When the ball is on a hashmark and inside the 10-yard line, the field goal unit may consider a "tackle over" call. This call will be made by the coach on the sideline and then is repeated in the huddle by the holder. The tackle that "comes over" will need to change his stance to his "inside hand down". Both the *ends* and *wings* are still eligible receivers. NOTE: The *holder* and *kicker* must be alert to an outside block from the boundary side. When this occurs, the spot must be moved a foot inside the hashmark.

"FIRE CALL":

- In the event of a malfunction, the holder and kicker should yell, "fire, fire."

- Interior linemen must be alert to stay on the LOS and continue to block their area, since this play will probably be a forward pass.

- The holder should field the ball and should roll right or left with a run-pass option.

- The wingbacks and ends should quickly release off their blocks to run the pattern diagrammed in Diagram 8-6. If the holder is scrambling with the ball, the wingbacks and ends should work toward an open area and wave their arms.

Diagram 8-5. Tackle-over field goal alignments.

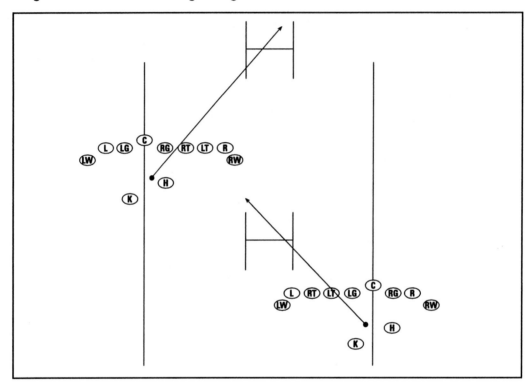

Diagram 8-6. "FIRE" call execution.

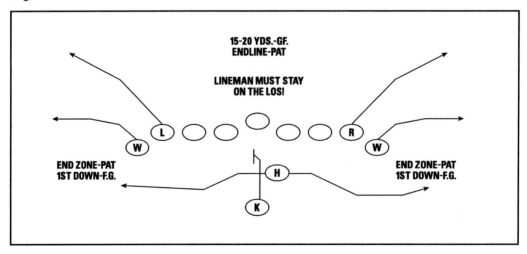

REMINDERS:

- The total time for the snap and kick must be 1.3 seconds or less.

- On a field goal attempt, the field-goal unit members must work quickly since the 25-second clock is running.

- Proper coverage on long field goals is imperative (treated like a punt).

- Unit members should be alert for "FIRE" calls.

- All missed field goals that do not travel into the end zone should be downed.

- Unit members should be alert for an audible (from "fake" to "kick").

- During the last two minutes of the second and fourth quarters, everyone should be alert on the sidelines, and near the head coach, where they can get into the game quickly. A "scramble" call may be instituted on the sideline – NO HUDDLE!

- The holder should let the clock run down to four seconds before calling for the snap. The ball should be snapped on "SET". Everyone should freeze in their stance until the ball is snapped (i.e., see the ball snapped).

FIELD GOAL PUNT-RIGHT:

- Block first – then cover

- Expect a return

- Down the ball

Diagram 8-7. Field-goal, punt-right assignments.

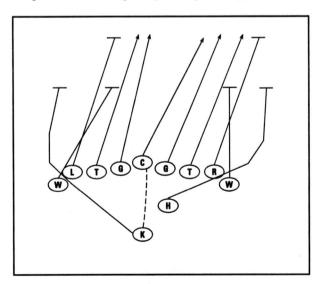

BLOCKING VARIATIONS:

- "DOWN" CALL BY THE END. (Diagram 8-8). When the end is clearly uncovered and there is only one rusher outside of him, a "down" call can be made. In this situation, the end should block down on the first man to his inside. The tackle can expect help and can secure his inside gap tougher. The wing-back should block the outside rusher man-to-man.

- "OUT" CALL BY THE END. (Diagram 8-9). When the tackle-end gap is clearly unthreatened and there are only two rushers on or outside the end, an "out" call can be made. The end should block the second man in man-to-man, while the wingback should block the outside rusher man-to-man.

Diagram 8-8. blocking adjustments on a "down" call by the end.

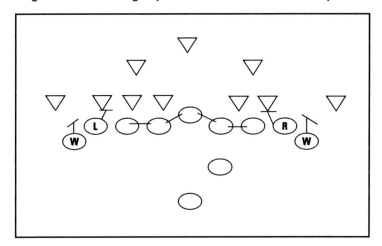

Diagram 8-9. Blocking adjustments on an "out" call by the end.

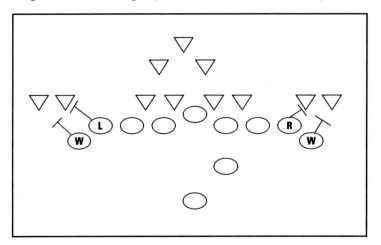

Diagram 8-10. Field goal coverage assignments for the kicking team.

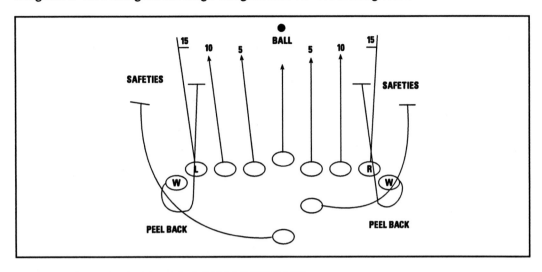

FIELD GOAL AND EXTRA POINT DEFENSE

Extra points and field goals are kicked in most games. Regardless of how much a team practices the "rush-and-block" area of the game, they will be unsuccessful at times. However, to be successful, the FG and PAT defense unit must concern itself with several factors. It must always be fundamentally sound as far as alignment and responsibilities are concerned, including: rushers rushing, blockers blocking, cover people covering, and everyone alert for fakes. It must perform when the pressure is on (i.e., when a kick means victory or defeat). This unit must stop all fakes with alertness and aggressiveness. Furthermore, everyone on this unit must know the rules pertaining to blocks, kicks, etc. They must constantly pressure the kicker and always attempt to block, and at the very least, harass each kick. Finally, they should be notorious for blocking kicks!

THE CALLS:

- The "CALL" will be signaled to the field captain from the sideline. He should make the call in the defensive huddle. NOTE: If the field-goal team does not huddle, the field captain should yell the call (scramble situation).

- Possible calls include:

  ❑ Block right

  ❑ Block left

  ❑ Double pinch

FG – PAT BLOCK PRINCIPLES

Everyone should:

- Be ready! Always be alert for a FAKE. Call it out!

- Know their alignment and assignment responsibilities.

- Go all out! They never know when one or three points will make the difference in the game.

- Know their "pass" responsibilities.

- Know who has "contain run" responsibilities.

- Stay onsides and get off on the snap! (See the ball in their stance.)

- Blocked kicks are treated the same as a blocked punt. Know the rules.

- Block the ball with their hands. Timing is important.

- Pick up and run with blocked balls that haven't crossed the LOS, i.e., "scoop and score."

- Tackle the opponent if they should pick up a blocked kick.

OUTSIDE BLOCKERS TECHNIQUES

Outside blockers should:

- Align as close to the LOS as possible. Use a sprinter's stance.

- Get off on the snap. Watch the snapper for tips, e.g., moving his fingers, tightens his grip on the ball, lifts the ball, bounces his butt or knees, has a rhythm after the "SET" call.

- Run as close to the wing as possible. Keep their shoulder level low. After their second outside step, drive flat for the ball. Accelerate hard to the block point, and keep their eyes on the ball.

- On the fourth or fifth step (depending on their stance), lay out flat across the path of the ball, turning their body in slightly.

- The ball should be blocked 4-5 feet from the ground with both hands. The block point is three yards in front of the spot.

BLOCK RIGHT

Diagram 8-11. Block right assignments.

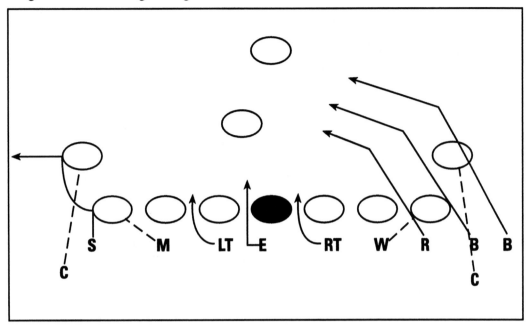

STANCE, ALIGNMENT, AND ASSIGNMENTS:

- OUTSIDE BLOCKER. Align outside the wing in a three-point stance. Rush through the groin of the wing to block point. SELL OUT FOR THE BLOCK!

- INSIDE BLOCKER. Align outside the TE in a three-point stance. Rush through the groin of the TE. If wing blocks him, he takes him with him down the LOS. If no contact, he continues to his block point. SELL OUT! (Use jump technique).

- RUSH. Align inside shade of the TE in a three-point stance. On a "BLOCK RIGHT" call, he rushes through the groin of the tackle to the block point.

- RIGHT TACKLE. Align in a 2 technique. Pinch through the A gap.

- END. Align in a 0 technique. Stem to the A gap away from the call. Jet through the A gap. SELL OUT!

- LEFT TACKLE. Align in a 2 technique. Loop to the B gap.

- SAM. Align outside shade of the TE in a three-point stance. Charge through the wing's outside shoulder to contain, as well as pick up, a blocked kick.

- <u>MIKE & WILLIE.</u> Align in a three-point stance in a 4 technique. Draw the OT's block; cover the TE to his side man-for-man.

- <u>CORNERS.</u> Align away from the block on the LOS in a three-point stance. Cover the wings man-for-man. The inside corner should move on the first sound and cover the wing to the blocked side (right).

BLOCK LEFT

Diagram 8-11. Block left assignments.

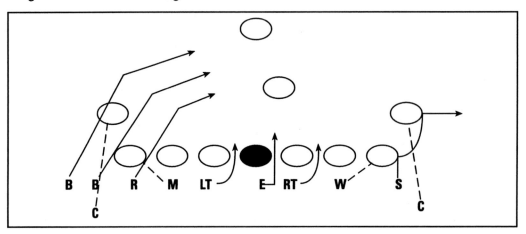

STANCE, ALIGNMENT, AND ASSIGNMENTS:

- <u>OUTSIDE BLOCKER.</u> Align outside the wing in a three-point stance. Rush through the groin of the wing to the block point. SELL OUT FOR THE BLOCK!

- <u>INSIDE BLOCKER.</u> Align outside the TE in a three-point stance. Rush through the groin of the TE. If the wing blocks him, he takes him with you down the LOS. If no contact occurs, he continues to his block point. SELL OUT! (Use the jump technique).

- <u>RUSH.</u> Align in an inside shade of the TE in a three-point stance. On a "BLOCK LEFT" call, he rushes through the groin of the tackle to the block point.

- <u>RIGHT TACKLE.</u> Align in a 2 technique. Loop through the B gap.

- <u>END.</u> Align in a 0 technique. Stem to the A gap away from the call. Jet through the A gap. SELL OUT!

- <u>LEFT TACKLE.</u> Align in a 2 technique. Pinch to the A gap.

- <u>SAM.</u> Align in an outside shade of the TE in a three-point stance. Charge through the wing's outside shoulder to contain, as well as pick up, a blocked kick.

- <u>MIKE & WILLIE.</u> Align in a three-point stance in a 4 technique. Draw the OT's block; cover the TE to his side man-for-man.

- <u>CORNERS.</u> Align away from the block on the LOS in a three-point stance. Cover the wings man-for-man. The inside corner should move on the first sound and cover the wing to the blocked side (left).

DOUBLE PINCH

Diagram 8-12. Pinch assignments.

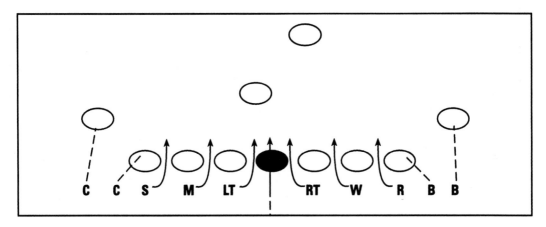

STANCE, ALIGNMENT, AND ASSIGNMENTS:

- <u>CORNERS.</u> Inside corner in man-for-man on the TE; outside corner man-for-man on the wing.

- <u>BLOCKERS.</u> Inside blocker man-for-man on the TE; outside blocker man-for-man on the wing.

- <u>MIKE & WILLIE.</u> Line up in 4 techniques. Pinch the B GAPS.

- <u>SAM & RUSH.</u> Line up in 6 techniques. Lightning the C GAPS.

- <u>TACKLES.</u> Line up in 2 techniques. Pinch the A GAP.

- <u>END.</u> Lines up 1.5 yards off the center. At the snap, the end should use a jump technique.

DEFENDING THE SWINGING GATE

Diagram 8-13. Assignments for defending the swinging gate.

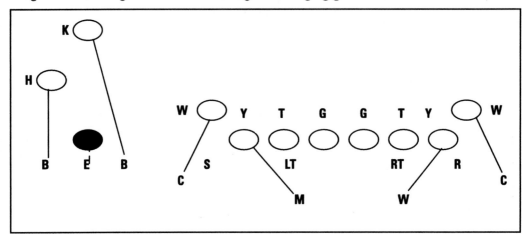

Everyone should be alert. If a team comes out in either a field goal or extra point situation and aligns in a formation on or near the LOS, the FG and PAT defensive unit should match-up with them in the following manner:

- Align across from the man they are responsible for covering in a "swinging gate" formation.

- Then, shift into the called block alignment as the opponent shifts back over to the ball.

NOTES:

- NOTES: If a wing or the center is aligned away from the huddle, the respective corner and nose must align with them. Remember the center may snap to the holder, kicker or a man behind the huddle. In addition, the holder or kicker may walk up and snap the ball.

MATCH UP (SWINGING GATE) ASSIGNMENTS:

- CORNERS: Man wings, and force

- BLOCKERS: Man holder and kicker

- MIKE: Man TE strongside

- WILLIE: Man TE weakside

- SAM & RUSH: Play the run; contain vs. pass

- END: Align on the center, man the center

- TACKLES: Play the run

Diagram 8-14. Common field-goal fakes.

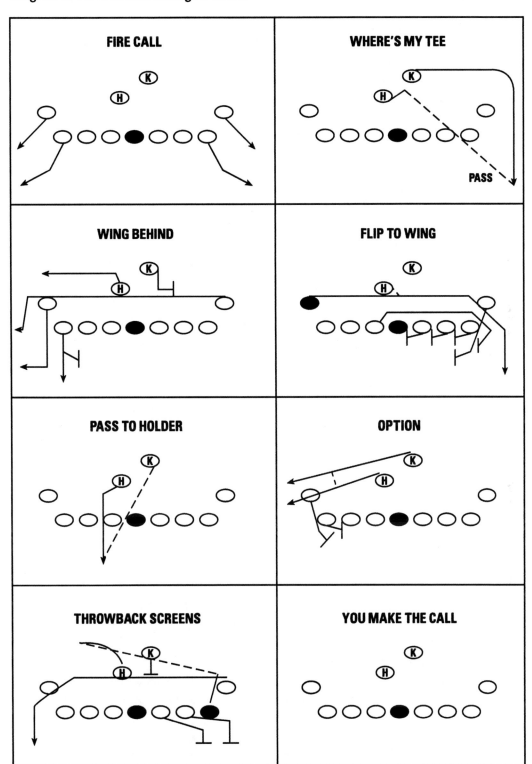

CHAPTER 9

SCOUTING REPORT AND GAME PLAN PREPARATION

As was discussed in chapter 2 ("Special Teams Organization"), paying attention to details will provide a team with the means of achieving the "winning edge." An essential aspect in this regard is to know what opponents are doing in the kicking game in order to prepare for that particular opponent. It is very important that enough time is spent to determine what the opponent has done in the past and what they might do in that particular game. Subsequently, it's incumbent upon the coaching staff to cover those situations so that there are no surprises come game day. Some coaching staffs are limited in terms of the number of coaches on the staff, by time constraints that might exist because of teaching responsibilities, and frequently by their limited video capabilities. Fortunately, however, most coaching staffs can take the guidelines set forth in this chapter and can benefit their teams by being more detailed in the game preparation of the special teams.

WEEKLY GAME PREPARATION

Weekly game preparation involves three general phases. The first phase is a study and analysis of the opponent's schemes and personnel. This phase can be done by "in-person scouting" or through game video study. It is suggested that coaches, as they study game tape of their opponent's schemes, make a list of plays to use in training tapes that will be shown to the individual kicking units during meetings in the week of preparation. Normally, this step would include four-to-six plays of each of the opponent's six kicking units. As an example, a coach right select four-to-six plays of the opponent's punt cover unit that would show their protection techniques, their protection rules against a variety of different punt returns and punt blocks, and their punt coverage. Another example might be to select four-to-six plays of the punt return unit that would show their punt returns and blocks, their alignment, how they try to block punts, and how they try to set up their punt returns.

For an opponent's kickoff cover unit, plays should be selected that show their basic alignment, the types of kicks that they execute: whether they're kicking the ball deep; whether they're squibing e.g., whether they're kicking it to the right side, to the left side, or any "bloops" (high and short kicks); and whether they kick from the middle or from the hashmarks? The training tape could also illustrate the variety of kickoff formations and kicks the opponent has used leading up to that point in time.

For an opponent's kickoff return unit, the coach should determine how many different returns the opponent has used and then put the most frequently used kickoff returns on the training tape. Also, how the opponent reacts to different types of kicks, like a squib or a bloop kick, and how prepared they are to handle those types of situations could be shown.

In addition, an opponent PAT and field-goal kick units could be evaluated. For example, do they go tackle-over or unbalanced on the hashmark, for instance? Do they have any fakes that they have shown from their PAT and field -goal formation? Do they use what is commonly referred to as the "swinging gate" scheme on PAT's, where they line up in a spread before shifting to their kick alignment? The PAT and field-goal defense unit should see the "swinging gate" in order to be fully prepared for any potential fake that might be run out of the "gate". And finally, a training tape could be made that would illustrate an opponent's various field-goal block schemes. This instructional tool could be shown to the field-goal unit. Subsequently, the unit could practice against those particular block schemes during the week. Again, some coaches may be limited in the number of tapes of an opponent they can study either during the week or on the weekend prior to the ball game. As a rule, however, it would not be too difficult to edit four-to-six plays of each of the opponent's kicking teams to show to a team's kicking units during game week. The "Special Teams Video Cut-Ups" form illustrated in Table 9-1 could be employed to help with this editing process.

The second phase of weekly game preparation is the development of a scouting report. The scouting report can be done through in-person scouting and/or through video game tape study. The sample scouting-report forms included in Appendix A illustrate one way to put the scouting report together.

Copies of the special team's scouting report, along with the game plan for each of those units, should be provided to the special teams personnel. As a result, they would have special teams scouting and game-plan materials, in addition to their offensive or defensive game-plan book, during the actual week of preparation for a particular opponent. As discussed earlier, the scouting report and game plan for special teams deserves the same attention to detail as offensive and defensive planning. But ultimately, the success of special teams units will depend on what each special team does and how well they do it. The prepared information must be transferred to the team on paper and on videotape, and then presented to the team in practice, and ultimately in the game situation.

Table 9-1. A sample special teams video cut-ups form.

SPECIAL TEAMS VIDEO CUT UPS

LABEL TAPE AS_____

Order	Recorded from	SL	EZ	Time Code	Heading

Once the scouting report is developed on paper, and training tapes are made of each of the opponent's six kicking units, the game plan can be formulated. Once the game plan has been developed, it is necessary during the game week to follow good teaching progressions. In fact, it is equally important to follow good teaching progressions during the season as it is in the pre-season. As a reminder, teaching progressions should include meetings, walk-throughs, practice and follow-up. For example, working with the punt cover unit might involve the following steps:

- Put the scouting report and game plan on transparencies to use for meetings.

- Show the training tape of the opponents most frequently used punt returns/blocks.

- Walk-through punt protections vs. opponents returns/blocks.

- Practice protections and coverage vs. opponents returns/blocks.

- Show and critique practice video.

In other words, the teaching progressions for special team units should parallel how the offense and defense are prepared.

In summary, the report given to players should be a combination scouting report/game plan. In reality, some coaches may not have the time to develop a scouting report as thoroughly as the one discussed and illustrated in this chapter and in Appendix A, or they may not have the time to develop the game plan as thoroughly as they might like. Hopefully, however, all coaches will be able to take many of these concepts presented in this chapter and use them with their special teams units to improve their performance.

The third phase of weekly game preparation is actually practicing the kicking game. This step involves practicing not only fundamentals and techniques, but also the game plan against an opponent's schemes. Similar to the other two phases, this phase is also essential. Keep in mind that, collectively, the three phases of game preparation are designed to thoroughly develop the kicking game plan for a particular opponent.

The execution of the scout teams during the kicking practice periods is critical to the success that special teams achieve on game day. While the role of the scout team coach and players has been discussed in other chapters, several points deserve repeated emphasis including:

- Have cards prepared for the opponents kicking game schemes.

- Communicate with scout team personnel so they know when, what, and where.

- The scout team coach should coach the scout team with enthusiasm.

- Try to use the same scout team personnel throughout the season to improve their learning curve.

- Practice "good-versus-good" whenever possible.

PRACTICE TIME

Coaching the scout teams takes extra time and effort, but the ultimate goal is to maximize limited practice time and help a team's special teams be successful. The "In-Season Meetings and Practice Schedule" presented in Table 9-2 provides a sample model to maximize meeting and practice time during the week— time that is almost always limited for special teams. With regard to making effective use of practice and meeting time, different models can be employed and used successfully. However, this model has been shown to work very well. It provides a team with the capability to practice and rehearse the situations in the kicking game that are needed during game week. This model is also designed to allow a team to go into a game with a lot of confidence because they realize that they are well prepared.

One of the most useful steps that a coach can undertake with regard to effective time management is to develop a detailed plan of how his team can best use their time on a daily basis during game week. In the example reviewed and discussed in this chapter, it is a Saturday game week. Thus, the starting point for a coach's game week planning efforts will be Sunday, which is the day after game day.

Sunday is a meeting and practice day. The special teams units meet at 4:15 p.m. with the special teams coordinator and those coaches who help with special teams. The head coach should be in attendance at that meeting also. Not all special teams players sit in on the entire 45-minute video session, but only for the time slots with which they are involved. As outlined, the punt cover, punt return, kickoff cover and kickoff return units meet during this 45-minute time period. Not all plays can be shown and critiqued in the time allotted. Therefore, on Sunday morning, the coach grading special teams should make a highlight video on each unit. Then, only a representative group of plays can be covered in detail. This way a good quality meeting with the big four special teams units can occur in a 45-minute period. At the conclusion of the special teams game video sessions, the head coach should have a team meeting with all team members where he will go over team goals and awards for the previous day's game. This includes special teams, particularly recognizing the special teams player of the game. Once this meeting has concluded, the team breaks into offensive and defensive unit and position meetings to review the game video. Field goal and field-goal block plays are reviewed in the offensive and defensive unit meetings.

After all meetings conclude, the team then practices in shorts and helmets only. After a good warm-up period, there is a 25-minute kicking period that is broken down into equal parts of punt cover and punt return/block. During the time allotted to punt cover, the emphasis is on fundamentals, footwork, releases, and coverage lanes. Then, during the time devoted to punt return/block, some punt block drills are conducted if they're needed at that particular stage of the season. The opponent's punt cover protection scheme will be introduced along with any adjustments to be made with the punt return/block unit for that particular week.

With this model, Monday is a day off for the players. There are no player meetings or practice. This approach allows the coaching staff to continue with the scouting report and game plan preparation.

Tuesday is a full-pads, practice day. The special teams scouting report and game plan book are ready to hand out. This material is put into the players' offensive and defensive game books so they will have those for the Tuesday meeting. Prior to practice on Tuesday, there will be a 15-minute kickoff cover meeting. In this 15-minute meeting, the scouting report and game plan for that week will be covered using transparencies and training videos.

Any adjustments and/or fakes from the PAT and field-goal protection will be inserted during the offensive unit meeting. Any adjustments that might have to be made by the PAT and field goal block unit are inserted during the defensive unit meeting.

Once on the practice field, the first thing that is done is a "kickoff-cover walk-through." This action will be a follow-up on the earlier meeting that day. The scout team has been prepared to show the two favorite kickoff returns of the opponent. The kickoff cover unit will walk and jog through their coverage lanes. This is done on one-half of the field. The kickoff cover unit will start from the 50-yard line. As they walk/jog, they visualize the drops and sets of the kickoff return unit. During the kickoff cover walk-through, the specialists not involved— punters, punt returners, PAT, field goal holders, kickers, snappers—will be working on another field.

About midway through the practice on Tuesday, there is a 15-minute kicking period. This 15-minute session is broken up into two periods—a five-minute live field goal-versus-field goal block session, followed by 10 minutes of punt return/block versus a scout punt team. The punt return/block unit will review their alignment and assignments through a combination of segment drills and full-team work. The scouting report of the opponent's punt protection and the basic game plan has previously been introduced in practice on Sunday afternoon.

Table 9-2. A sample in-season meetings and practice schedule.

SUNDAY	MONDAY	TUESDAY	WEDNESDAY	THURSDAY	FRIDAY	SATURDAY
Helmet & shorts	No player meetings or practice.	Pads	Pads	Shells	Shorts	

Game Video
4:15 Punt cover mtg..
4:30 Punt pressure mtg..
4:40 KO cover mtg..
4:50 KO return mtg..
5:00 Team mtg..
  1. Goals
  2. Awards
Including special teams
  1. Top gun (players of the game)
  2. Draw the line-KOC
  3. Coverage player
O/D Position mtgs..
Review game video
O/D Unit mtgs..
  1.FG & FG block
   Game video
  2. Goals & awards
  3. Begin scouting report
Team mtg..
Practice
10) Warm-up & stretch
10) Individual
25) Kick-PC (10), PP (15)
PC 1. 1/2 line-kick/slide release & form tackle
  2. Full cover & shoo chicken
  3. Sky drills
PP 1. Block Drills &/or segment drills
  2. Scout report (walk thru & game plan vs. opponent
10) Team
10) Conditioning
	Lift weights and use the training room if necessary.	Hand out special teams scouting reports and game book
		
		2:15 KO cover mtg.. (scout report and game plan)
		2:20 O/D-scout rpt.. & game plan
		
		Offense/Defense Unit
		5) PAT/FG scout Report
		  PAC/FG block Scout report
		15) Muscle
		  Team mtg..or early-outs (teach)
		1) Specialists period
		2) KOC walk-thru Practice
		  Warm-up & stretch Individual
		  Run drill –O vs. D
		
		15) Kick-FG vs FGB (5), PP (10)
		1) Alignment & assignment review
		2) Team segments
		3) Full team
		15) Kick FG vs. FGB (5), PP (10)
		  Group & skeley
		  Pass drill-O vs. D
		  Punt block vs. opponent (one play live)
		  Team group
		10) Conditioning
			2:15 KOR mtg.. (10) & PC mtg.. (10)
			  Scout rpt.. & game plan
			2:35 O/D mtgs..
			  Early outs (teach)
			  Specialists period
			Practice
			10) Warm-up & stretch
			  Individual run drill
			15) Kick-PC (15)
			1) 1/2 line
			2) TM review vs. opponent
			3) Fake
			4) Danger (live with full cover)
			  Group & Skeley
			  Pass drill-O vs. D
			  Three/live FGs
			  Team/group
			10) KOR & conditioning
				2:15 Kick mtg.. – KOC (10), PP (10)
				2:35, O/D mtgs..
				  Team mtg. or early outs
				  Practice
				10)Warm-up & stretch
				10) Individual
				25) Kick-PC (10), KOC(71/2), KOR(71/2)
				PC 1) Review vs opponent
				2) Fake
				3) Quick snap
				4) Sky & pooch vs safe
				KOC 1) Time-ups
				2)1/2 cover vs #1 return
				3) 1/2 cover vs #2 return
				4) Full cover vs air bloop KO
				5) Devil Sharks vs air
				KOR 1) vs onsides, squibs, bloops
				2) Game plan return #1
				3) Game plan return #2
				4) KOR after safety vs. punter
					Kick mtgs.., KOR (15), PC(15)
					  Team mtg.
					  To stadium
					  Practice substitution
					  Situation Script
					  Leave Stadium
					  Buses leave for dinner
					  Dinner
					  Arrive at hotel
					  O/D unit mtgs..
					  Team meetings
					  Snack
					  Lights out
						GAME DAY

Toward the end of practice and during some offense-versus-defense work (maybe a pass drill), a live punt block versus the scout punt team will be inserted. No specific time is allotted for this work—the head coach will "call it up" whenever he wants to. However, the scout team is prepared to take the field immediately at that point, so time will not be wasted.

Wednesday is a full-pads day of work. Prior to practice, two special teams meetings of 10 minutes each will be held. The first is a 10-minute kickoff return meeting, followed by a 10-minute, punt-cover meeting. In each meeting, a brief scouting report and game-plan presentation is made, again using previously prepared transparencies and training tapes. These meetings should be on time and very concise, since a lot of material must be covered in a relatively short period of time. Once the team is on the field, a 10-minute specialist period is conducted prior to practice. The kickers should already be on the field, warmed up and stretched, and ready to kick. Again, approximately halfway through practice, a 15-minute kicking period is held. This kicking period is all punt cover. Most of this period is half-line drills conducted at full speed against a live rush— in other words, against block attempts. Some release and short cover will be included, particularly when changing from one unit to the next. A "danger" punt situation will always be included at the end of this period. The ball is placed on the two-yard line, and the scout team is instructed to try to block the kick. The punt team will execute the kick and full cover, and then will wrap-up the returner. This is the only full cover for the punt cover unit on Wednesday. Since coverage lanes were reviewed on Sunday, and this is a hard practice day, any running should be limited during this kicking period.

At the end of practice on Wednesday, a 10-minute kickoff return period is conducted. The scout kickoff cover team is organized to provide two deep at every position. This two deep will reduce time between kicks, and thus, increase the number of repetitions performed. The returns will first be done by segment—front five drops and sets, and then the wedge and returners react and set up based upon the called return. Then, a full-team return with both the primary return and secondary return will be executed. This sequence is then repeated with the second unit. With this process, a lot of repetitions are performed in a relatively short period of time, because while one scout unit is covering, the second unit moves up and is prepared to kick and cover as quickly as the kickoff return team can reset.

Thursday's practice is generally in shells—helmets and shoulder pads. As the season progresses, sometimes the Thursday practice becomes just shorts and helmets. Two meetings are held prior to Thursday's practice. The first is a 10-minute kickoff cover meeting, followed by a 10-minute punt return/block meeting. These are the second meetings of the week for these two units and should feature the training tapes of the opponent's punt cover and kickoff returns.

During practice on Thursday, a 25-minute period is set aside just for kicking. The punt-cover, kickoff-cover, and kickoff-return units are rehearsed during these 25 minutes. Basically, the punt-cover unit will be full-team on this day, as opposed to the mostly half-line work done on Wednesdays. Protections are reviewed against the opponent's anticipated blocks and returns. Any fakes will be reviewed, and then the focus will be on working on full covering a sky or pooch kick with an attempt to down the ball inside the 10-yard line.

Next, the kickoff cover unit will execute a couple of "time-ups"—hitting the line altogether with the first unit and first kickoff man, followed by the second unit and second kickoff man. Both kicks involve a "short cover"—cover 10 yards downfield only. While working on time-ups, the scout kickoff return team is getting lined up and ready to show the opponent's favorite two kickoff returns. Then the kickoff cover unit will start from the 50-yard line to cover the returns. The emphasis is on proper coverage lanes and recognizing return indicators that have been covered in the scouting report and training tapes.

After covering the opponent's two favorite returns, the onside kick unit will rehearse the onside kick and recover against air (no return unit). This is done to avoid collisions because the players have no pads. While the onside kickoff is being rehearsed, the scout team is getting organized into a two-deep, kickoff-cover alignment. While the scout team is getting organized, two kickers assume a position on each hash of the 35-yard line. These two kickers will alternate kicking surprise onside kicks to the front five, and then squibs and bloops to the wedge unit and safety to the side of the kick. A lot of repetitions will occur in a short period of time by this method of alternating kicks from one hash to the other against one half of the kickoff return unit.

At that point, the scout team should be well organized and ready to kick and cover to the area, or areas, charted in the scouting report. The return team will execute full-team returns against the scout kickoff-cover teams. And, particularly early in the season, the kickoff return after a safety should be rehearsed versus both a place kicker and a punter. Versus a place kicker, the normal returners should remain in the game. However, if the opponent utilizes a punter, the kickoff returners should be replaced with the number one and number two punt returners.

On Fridays (the day before the game), the team dresses in shorts only. This model has two special teams meetings in the afternoon on Fridays, whether or not the game is at home or away. Some models have a 30-minute "big four" meeting featuring training video. The two-meeting model would include kickoff-return and punt-cover units. These meetings would be the second of the week for those units. In addition, field goal and field-goal block procedures are reviewed in Friday's offensive and defensive unit meetings. Thus, all six kicking units are covered in at least two meetings per week.

On Fridays, the team will also go to the stadium and walk through a substitution/situation script, which involves not only specific offensive and defensive situations, but also kicking situations in order to review and become thoroughly acquainted with the proper substitution and calls made at the appropriate time. This scenario provides an excellent rehearsal/preparation for game day. Table 9-3 illustrates a sample "Situation Game-Day Script" for this practice.

At the end of practice on Friday, a good opportunity exists to rehearse the 10 perfect kicks. The number one field goal snapper, holder, and kicker should kick 10 balls from different positions on the field. The coach should expect 10 perfect kicks from that unit. Also, the long snapper and punter, and punt returners, should be on another field rehearsing two situations. First, they kick six sky punts. The managers place six balls in a row, starting on the +38-yard line to the +44-yard line. The first snap would be the ball placed on the 44-yard line, and then work toward the goal line one ball at a time. The punter attempts to punt the ball inside the 10-yard line, while the punt returners use good communication in either fielding the ball outside the 10-yard line, or letting the ball hit and roll into the end zone if it is kicked inside the 10-yard line.

Then, after six kicks, the snapper and punter switch to the danger situation by placing the ball on the two-yard line. At this point, the coach should time the snapper and punter to make sure that the ball is kicked in no more than 1.8 seconds. Four kicks should be made from that situation to the punt returners. These kicks conclude the 10 perfect kick session on Friday.

Saturday is game day. A normal pre-game warm-up situation should include all kicking specialists—kickoff, kickoff returners, field goal snappers, holders, kickers, and punt snappers, punters, and punt returners. This session is usually completed before the remainder of the team takes the field for their pre-game warm-up.

This concludes the weekly schedule—meetings, walk-throughs, and practice for the special teams during the season. Obviously, some adjustments will be made during bye weeks, or early in Bowl-game or post-season preparation efforts. At that time, it is a good approach to go back and practice some of the fundamental and technique work that was used early in fall camp, when the kicking game was initially introduced. Such a review of fundamentals and techniques is necessary because the kicking game is often under-practiced at these times. Thus, this review may very well provide a team with the "winning edge."

Table 9-3. A sample situation game-day script.

TEAM/KICKING SCRIPT/SITUATION		
TEAM	KICKING SCRIPT	SITUATION
Kickoff Return	35 (M)	Opening Kickoff
Offense	-32 (M)	1st + 10
Punt Team	-40 (L)	4th Down
Defense	+30 (R)	3rd + 5
Punt Return	+35 (R)	4th Down
Kickoff (Deep)	35 (Hash)	Kickoff
Defense	50 (L)	1st + 10
1st Offense vs. 1st Defense	+20 (M)	2nd Down
Scramble FG & FG Block	+20 (L)	Running out of Time
HALF-TIME		
Defense	50 (M)	3rd + Down
"Safe" Team vs. Fake	50 (M)	4th Down
"Safe Team" vs. Punt		
Punt (Danger) & Take Safety (Two Snaps)	-2(L)	4th Down
Defense – GOAL LINE	+2 (R)	
Field Goal Block – OPP (Blocked Kick)	+30 (R)	4th Down
Offense (Muscle)	+4 (R)	Goal Line
PAT	+3 (M)	PAT
Hands Team (Infield Practice)	35 (M)	Kickoff Return
Defense – VICTORY	50 (M)	
Offense – VICTORY	50 (M)	

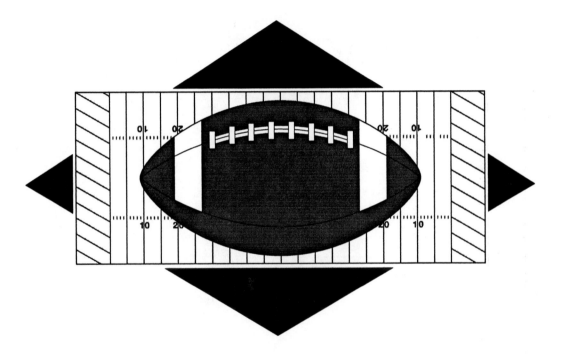

Diagram A-1a. A sample scouting (opponent) punt return/block team form.

SCOUTING (OPPONENT) PUNT RETURN/BLOCK TEAM

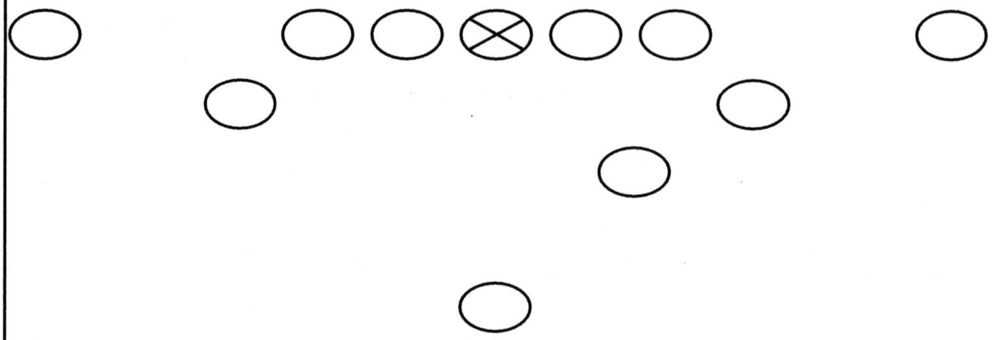

I. SYSTEM ANALYSIS: _____
   A. RETURNS: _____
   _____
   _____
   _____
   B. BLOCKS: _____
   _____
   _____
   C. SHIFTING: _____
   _____
   _____
   D. REVERSE: _____
   _____
   _____

II. STATISTICS: <u>NO   AVG   TD   LONG</u> _____
   _____
   _____
   _____
   TOTALS: _____

III. RETURNERS: _____ #____
   _____ #____
   A. ALIGNMENT: _____
   B. ACCELERATION: _____
   C. SPEED: _____
   D. FIELD ABILITY: _____
   E. COURAGE: _____
   F.º QUALITY SUMMARY: _____

IV. KEY OBSERVATIONS: _____
   _____
   _____
   _____

V. DO THEY MASS SUBSTITUTE? _____
VI. HAVE THEY BLOCKED ANY PUNTS? _____
   HOW? _____
   _____
   _____
   WHEN? _____
   _____

Diagram A-1b. A completed scouting (opponent) punt return/block team form.

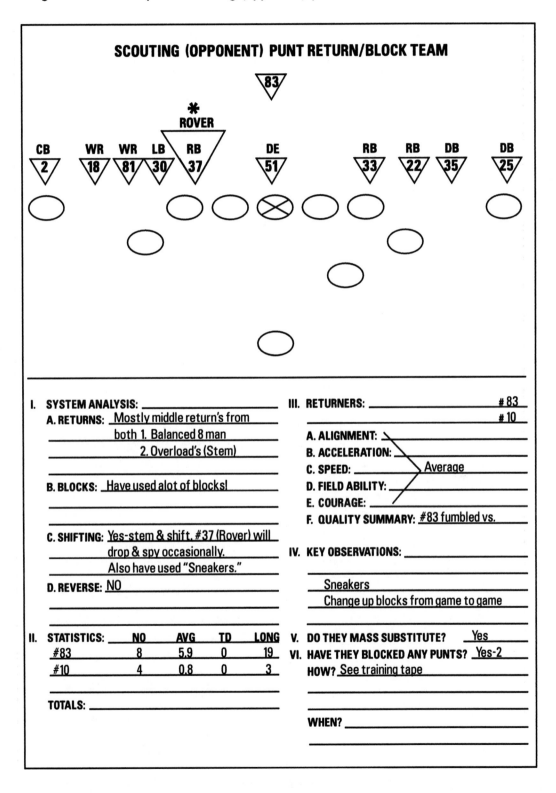

SCOUTING (OPPONENT) PUNT RETURN/BLOCK TEAM

I. **SYSTEM ANALYSIS:** _____
   A. **RETURNS:** _Mostly middle return's from_
   _____ both 1. Balanced 8 man
   _____ 2. Overload's (Stem)
   _____

   B. **BLOCKS:** _Have used alot of blocks!_
   _____

   C. **SHIFTING:** _Yes-stem & shift. #37 (Rover) will_
   _____ drop & spy occasionally.
   _____ Also have used "Sneakers."

   D. **REVERSE:** NO _____
   _____

II. **STATISTICS:**

	NO	AVG	TD	LONG
#83	8	5.9	0	19
#10	4	0.8	0	3

   TOTALS: _____

III. **RETURNERS:** _____ # 83
   _____ # 10
   A. **ALIGNMENT:** _____
   B. **ACCELERATION:** _____
   C. **SPEED:** ⟩ Average
   D. **FIELD ABILITY:** _____
   E. **COURAGE:** _____
   F. **QUALITY SUMMARY:** #83 fumbled vs.

IV. **KEY OBSERVATIONS:** _____
   _____
   _____ Sneakers
   _____ Change up blocks from game to game
   _____

V. **DO THEY MASS SUBSTITUTE?** _Yes_

VI. **HAVE THEY BLOCKED ANY PUNTS?** _Yes-2_
   HOW? _See training tape_
   _____
   _____
   WHEN? _____
   _____

Diagram A-2a. A sample scouting (opponent) punt team form.

SCOUTING (OPPONENT) PUNT TEAM

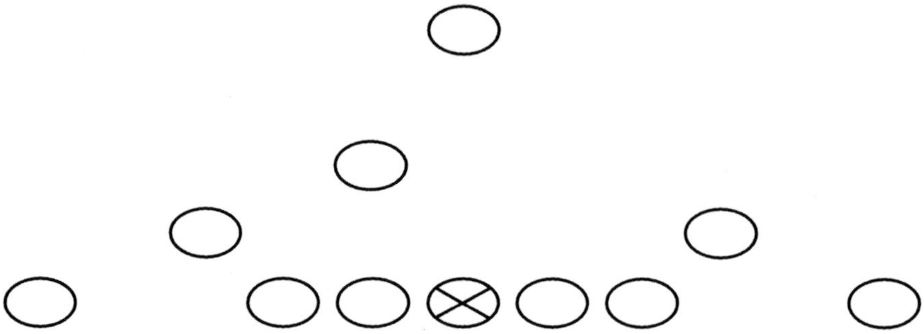

I. SYSTEM ANALYSIS: _____
_____
_____
_____
_____

II. PROTECTION: _____
   A. OVERALL QUALITY: _____
   B. BLOCK TECHNIQUE: _____
   C. WEAKNESS: _____
   _____
   D. OUR BLOCK POINT: _____

III. KEY OBSERVATIONS: _____
_____
_____
_____
_____
_____

IV. SNAPPER: _____ # _____
_____
_____
_____

V. PUNTER: _____ # _____
   A. ALIGNMENT: _____
   B. RT/LT FOOTED: _____
   C. APPROACH: _____
   D. STEPS: _____
   E. GET OFF TIME: _____
   F. HANG TIME: _____
   G. PUNT AVG: _____
   H. SKY PUNT?: _____
   I. CORNER KICKER?: _____
   J. STATISTICS: _NO_ _AVG_ _LT TB FC 120 BLKD_
   _____

VI. NET PUNT AVERAGE: _____
_____
_____
_____
_____

VII. COVERAGES: _____
   A. MISSILES: _____ # _____
   _____ # _____
   B. SPEED: _____
   C. CONVERGENCE: _____
   D. OVERALL QUALITY: _____
   _____
   _____

VIII. ANY PUNTS BLOCKED? _____
   HOW? _____
   _____
   WHEN? _____
   _____

Diagram A-2b. A completed scouting (opponent) punt team form.

SCOUTING (OPPONENT) PUNT TEAM

(87)

RB   #8
(37)   *#31   or
RB   #48   or   WR
(34)   or   *   (35)
CB   LB   DE   OC   DE   RB   WR
(25)   (57) (51) (X) (6) (22)   (18)

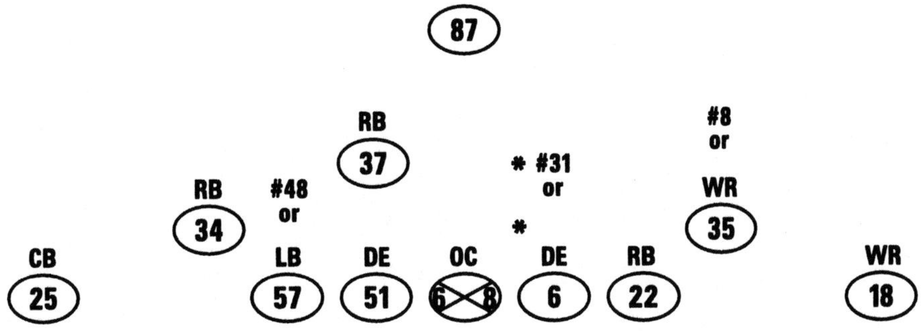

I. SYSTEM ANALYSIS: Larry/Roger

*FB taps the snapper on LT or RT hip
to tell him which way to protect

II. PROTECTION:
A. OVERALL QUALITY: Good
B. BLOCK TECHNIQUE: Kick/Slide
C. WEAKNESS:

D. OUR BLOCK POINT: 10 yds. directly behind
snapper

III. KEY OBSERVATIONS:

1. Punter offset to RT A-Gap and steps
back to middle

2. Snapper is a slow cover guy!

IV. SNAPPER: #68

*DG: 6-4, 275

V. PUNTER: #87
A. ALIGNMENT: 14-14 1/2
B. (RT)/LT FOOTED:
C. APPROACH: Offset to RT A-Gap
D. STEPS: 2
E. GET OFF TIME: 2.1-2.2
F. HANG TIME: 3.9-4.0
G. PUNT AVG: 40.8
H. SKY PUNT?: No
I. CORNER KICKER?: Yes
J. STATISTICS:

NO	AVG	LT	TB	FC	I20	BLKD
31	40.8	60	0	6	8	0

TOTALS:
VI. NET PUNT AVERAGE: 36.8
18 Returns: 6.9 avg.; LG 23 yds.

VII. COVERAGES:
A. MISSILES: (SR/CB) # 39
(SO/WR) # 18
B. SPEED:
C. CONVERGENCE: > Good
D. OVERALL QUALITY: /

VIII. ANY PUNTS BLOCKED? Bad snap vs.   & punter
HOW? Tackled after getting first down

WHEN?

Diagram A-3a. A sample punter's (opponent) hit chart.

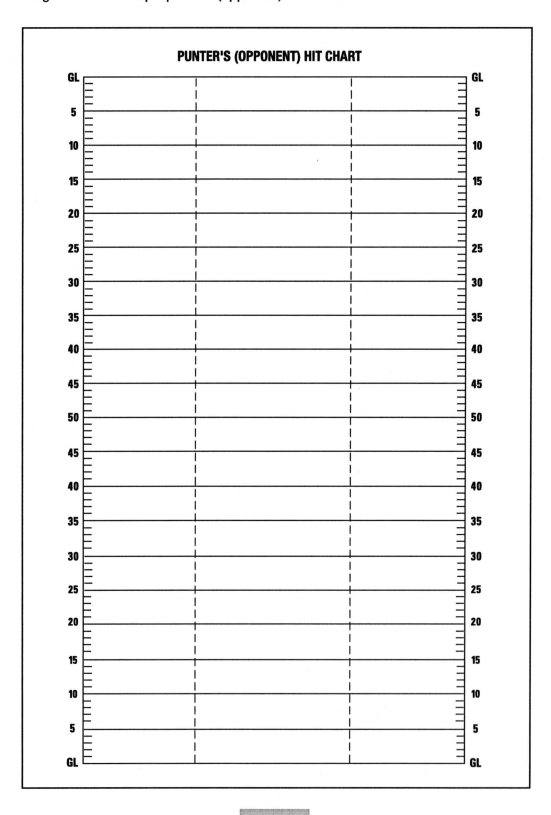

Diagram A-3b. A completed punter's (opponent) hit chart (for two games).

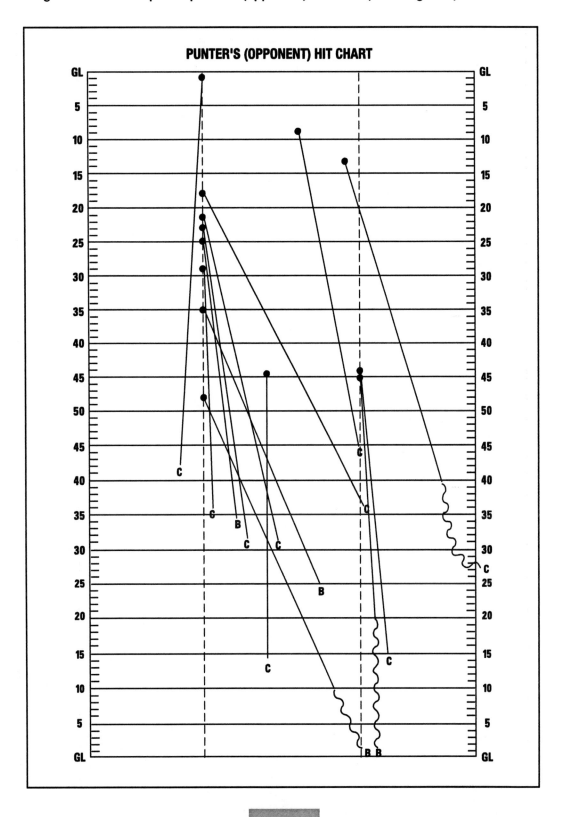

Diagram A-4a. A sample punt-cover (opponent) lanes chart.

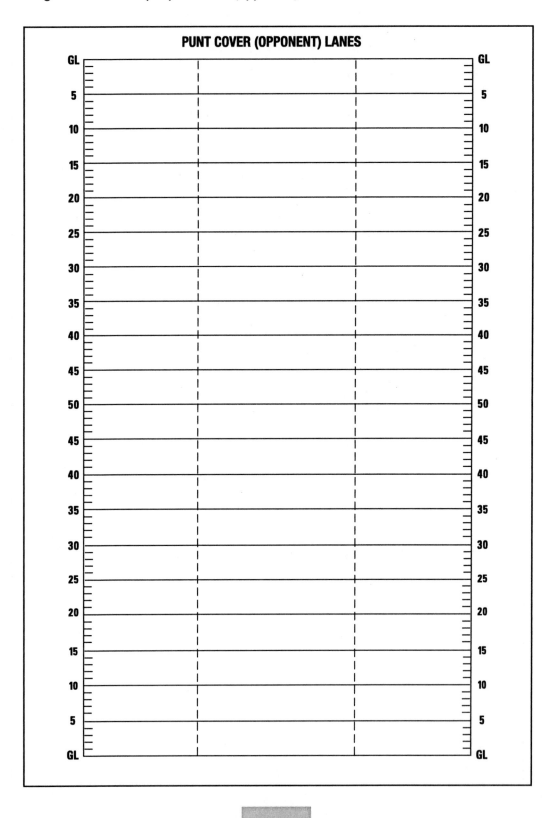

Diagram A-4b. A completed punt-cover (opponent) lanes chart.

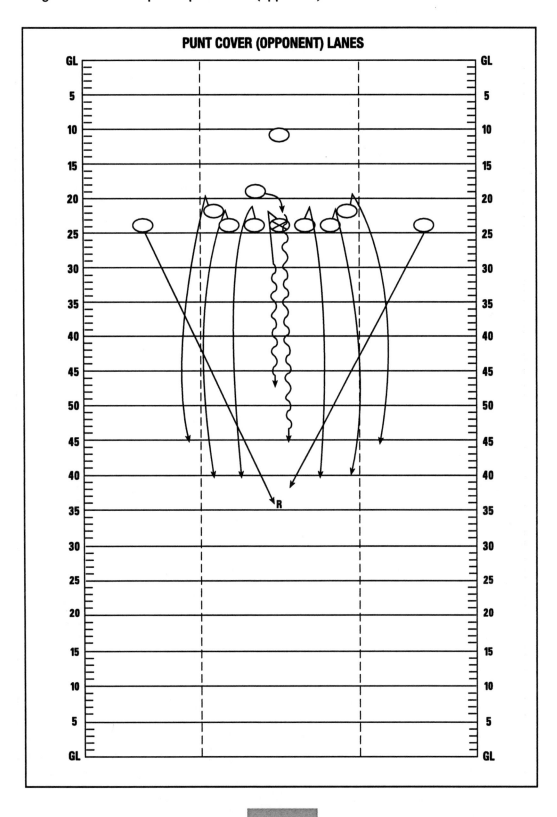

PUNT COVER (OPPONENT) LANES

Diagram A-5a. A sample scouting (opponent) kickoff return team form.

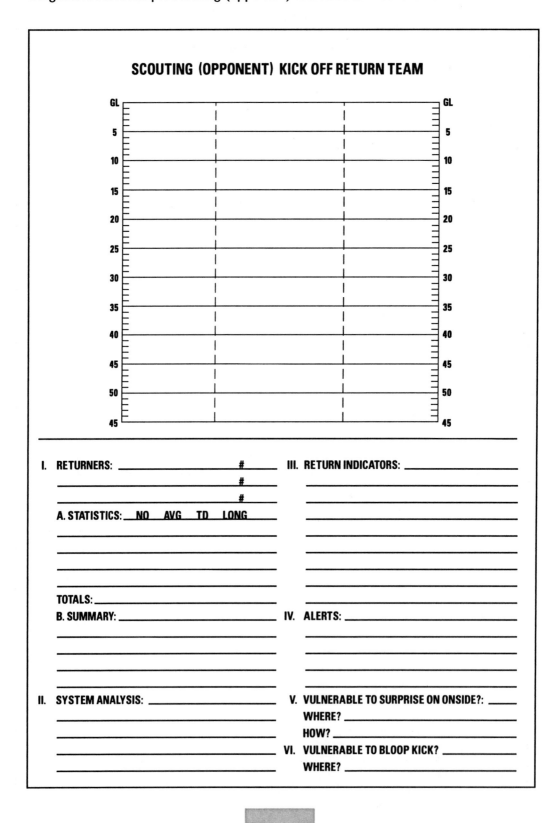

SCOUTING (OPPONENT) KICK OFF RETURN TEAM

I. RETURNERS: _____ # _____
    _____ # _____
    _____ # _____
    A. STATISTICS: __NO__ __AVG__ __TD__ __LONG__
    _____
    _____
    _____
    _____
    TOTALS: _____
    B. SUMMARY: _____
    _____
    _____
    _____

II. SYSTEM ANALYSIS: _____
    _____
    _____
    _____
    _____

III. RETURN INDICATORS: _____
    _____
    _____
    _____
    _____
    _____
    _____
    _____

IV. ALERTS: _____
    _____
    _____
    _____

V. VULNERABLE TO SURPRISE ON ONSIDE?: _____
    WHERE? _____
    HOW? _____

VI. VULNERABLE TO BLOOP KICK? _____
    WHERE? _____

Diagram A-5b. A completed scouting (opponent) kickoff return team form.

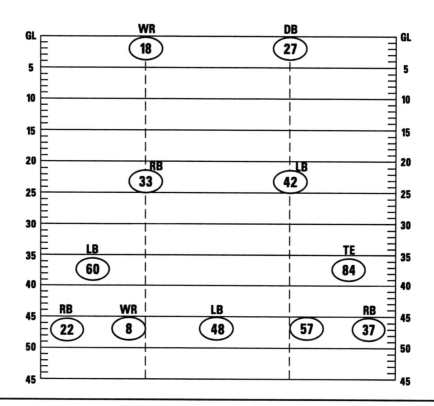

SCOUTING (OPPONENT) KICK OFF RETURN TEAM

I. **RETURNERS:**
(SO/WR) # 18
(FR/CB) # 27
(SR/SAF) # 10

A. STATISTICS:

	NO	AVG	TD	LONG
#18	9	15.7	0	19
#27	6	24.2	0	40
#10	5	25.2	0	38
TOTALS:	20	20.6	0	40

B. SUMMARY: _____

II. **SYSTEM ANALYSIS:** _____
1. Veer/Wedge Returns
2. Trap Returns w/Double Team on #3 to
   Return Side
   *Do Not Convert-stay with called return
   regardless of where ball is kicked.

III. **RETURN INDICATORS:** _____
Veer/Wedge Returns
1. Setup & Angle of Wedge
2. Drop angles of Front 5

Trap Returns
1. HB & End to side of return DT #3
2. HB & End to backside of return run across
   to trap #1 & #2 to return side.

IV. **ALERTS:** _____
1. Wide field Returns
2. Trap Returns

V. **VULNERABLE TO SURPRISE ON ONSIDE?:** No
WHERE? _____
HOW? _____

VI. **VULNERABLE TO BLOOP KICK?** Yes
WHERE? _____

Diagram A-6a. A sample opponent's kickoff return chart.

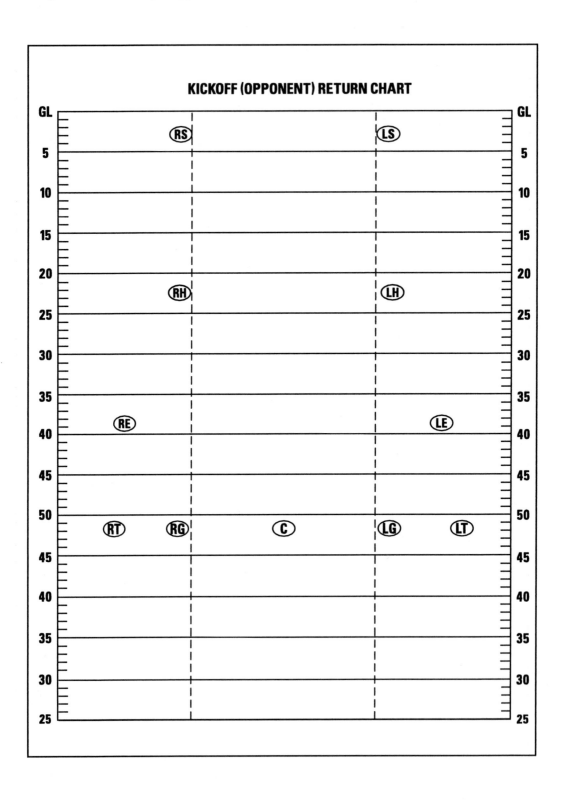

Diagram A-6b. A completed opponent's kickoff return chart (veer right).

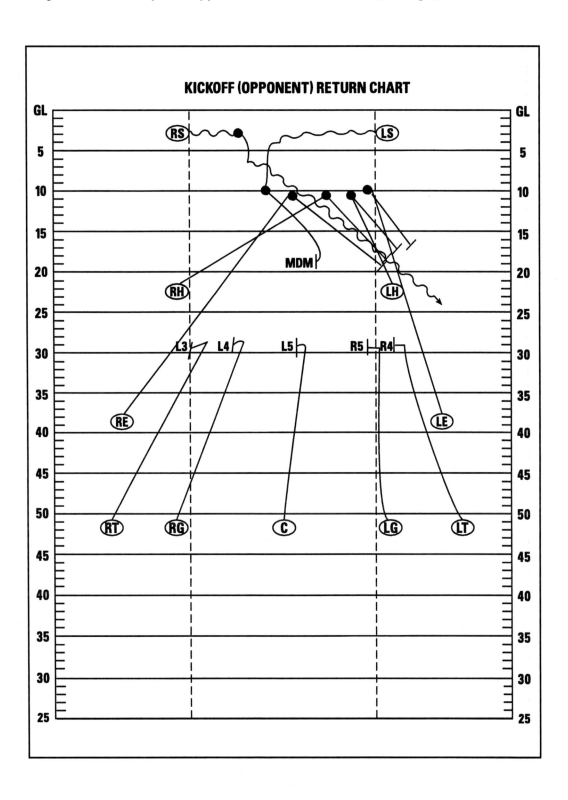

Diagram A-7a. A sample scouting (opponent) kickoff coverage team form.

SCOUTING (OPPONENT) KICKOFF COVERAGE TEAM

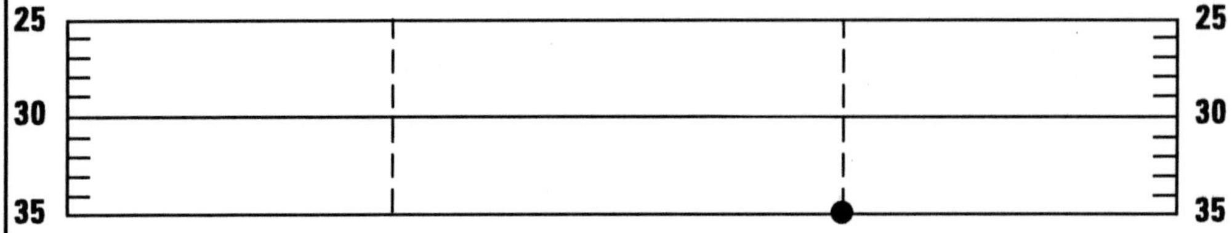

I. SYSTEM ANALYSIS: _____
_____
_____
_____

II. COVERAGE: _____
_____
_____
_____

III. BEST COVER MEN:
_____ # _____
_____ # _____
_____ # _____

IV. SAFETIES:
_____ # _____
_____ # _____
_____ # _____

V. AVERAGE RETURN VS. THEM: _____
VI. AVERAGE START LINE VS. THEM: _____
_____

VII. KICKER: _____ #
A. APPROACH: _____
B. DIRECTION: _____
C. HANG TIME: _____
D. DISTANCE: _____
E. RT/LT FOOTED: _____
F. ONSIDE ABILITY: _____
_____

VIII. KEY OBSERVATIONS: _____
1. _____
2. _____
3. _____

IX. ONSIDE KICKS:
A. SCORE OF GAME: _____
B. TIME REMAINING: _____
C. SURPRISE? _____
D. ALIGNMENT: _____

Diagram A-7b. A completed scouting (opponent) kickoff coverage team form.

SCOUTING (OPPONENT) KICKOFF COVERAGE TEAM

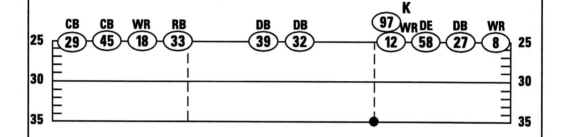

I. **SYSTEM ANALYSIS:** The last 3 games have KO'd from own LT Hash to RT Safety, the 1st 3 games KO'd to middle & scattered all over the field.

II. **COVERAGE:** Very good speed & aggressive

III. **BEST COVER MEN:**
   3 position # 58
   2 position # 27
   5 position # 32

IV. **SAFETIES:**
   Kicking # 97
   #10 position # 29
   #

V. **AVERAGE RETURN VS. THEM:** 21.2

VI. **AVERAGE START LINE VS. THEM:**
   31 Returns/LG = 53 yds.

VII. **KICKER:** (SR/K) # 97
   A. **APPROACH:** 9 X 3
   B. **DIRECTION:** see hit chart
   C. **HANG TIME:**
   D. **DISTANCE:** see hit chart
   E. (RT) LT **FOOTED:**
   F. **ONSIDE ABILITY:**

VIII. **KEY OBSERVATIONS:**
   1. #9 position peels
   2. #10 will be safety or cover outside #8
   3. Last 3 games have KO'd from own LT Hash

IX. **ONSIDE KICKS:**
   A. **SCORE OF GAME:** behind
   B. **TIME REMAINING:** late in game (4th Quarter)
   C. **SURPRISE?** No
   D. **ALIGNMENT:** see below

Diagram A-8a. A sample opponent's kickoff cover hit chart.

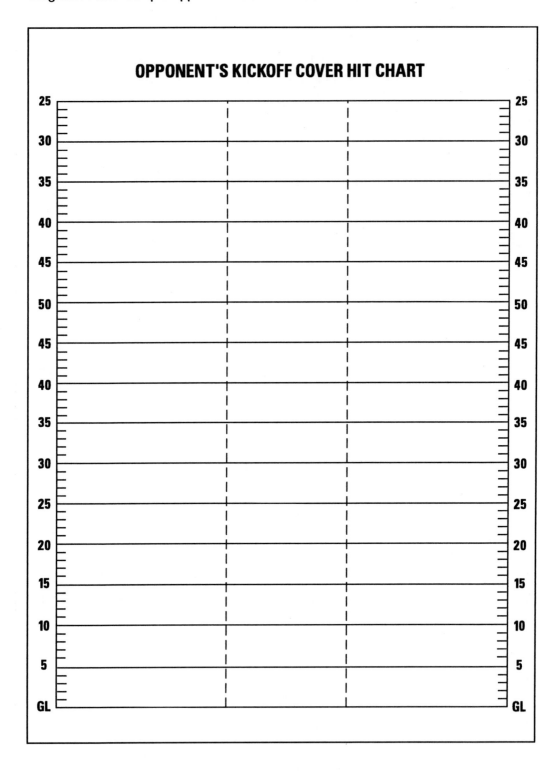

Diagram A-8b. A completed opponent's kickoff cover hit chart.

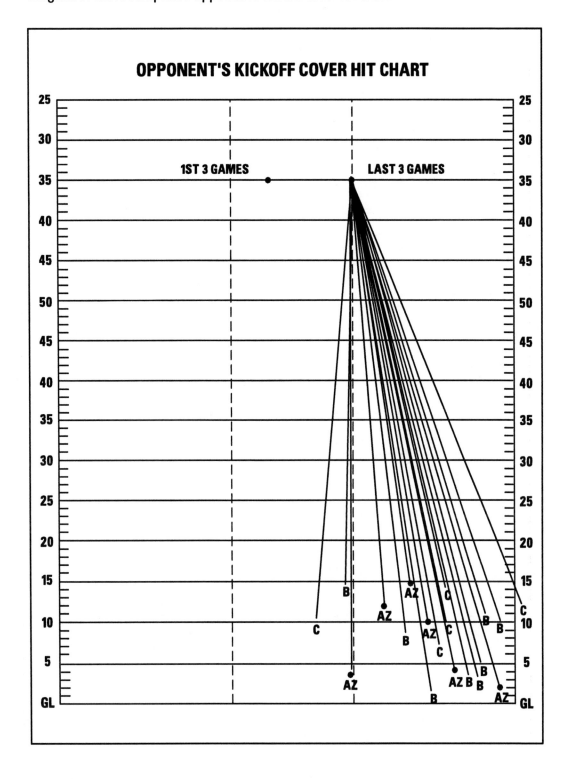

Diagram A-9a. A sample opponent's kickoff cover lanes chart.

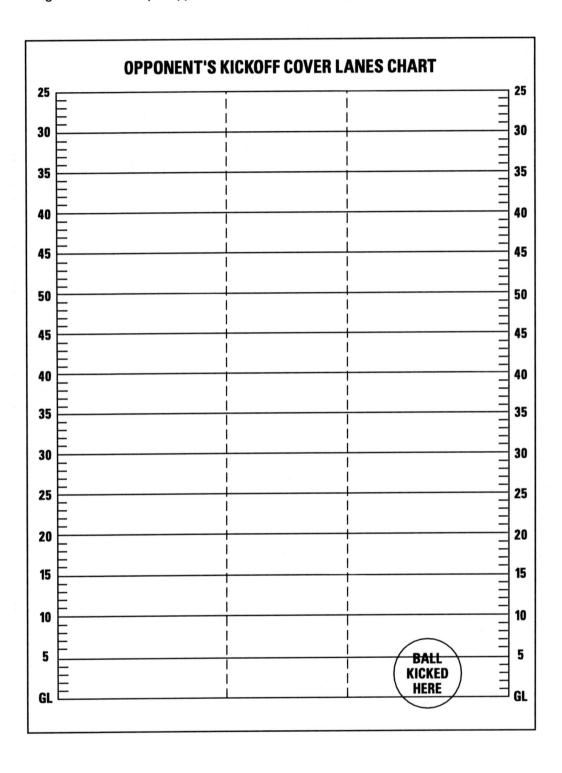

Diagram A-9b. A completed opponent's kickoff cover lanes chart.

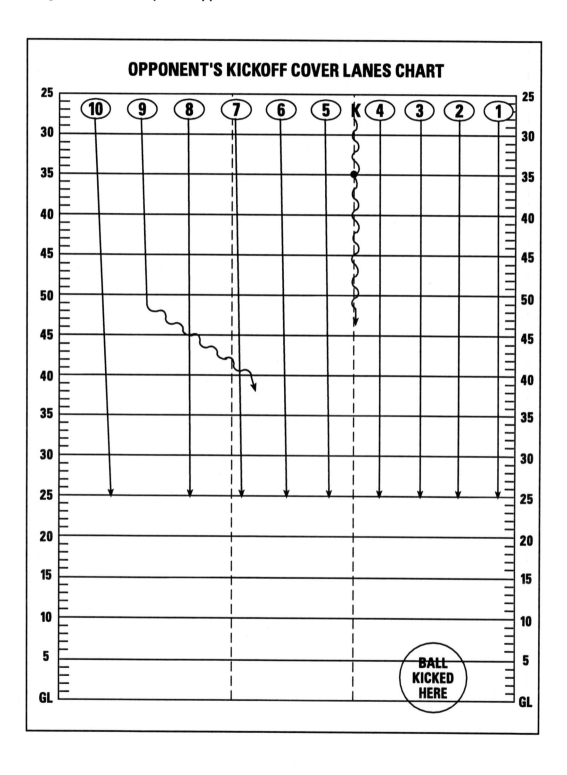

Diagram A-10a. A sample scouting (opponent) field goal/PAT team form.

SCOUTING (OPPONENT) FIELD GOAL/PAT TEAM

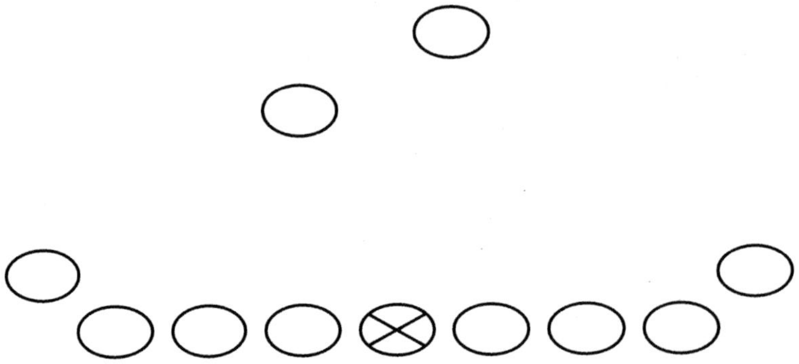

I.   **PROTECTION SCHEME:**_____
    A. LINE: _____
    B. ENDS: _____
    C. WINGS: _____
    _____

II. **A. STRENGTHS:** _____
    _____
    _____
    _____
    B. WEAKNESSES: _____
    _____
    _____
    _____

III. **HOLDER:** _____ #_____
    _____
    TEE IS PLACED: _____
IV. **SNAPPER:** _____ #_____
    _____
V.   **WINGS ELIGIBLE?** _____
VI. **ENDS ELIGIBLE?** _____
VII. **HOW DO WE BLOCK?** _____

VIII. **KICKER:** _____
    A. RT/LT FOOTED: _____
    B. STEPS: _____
    C. GET OFF TIME: _____
    D. KICK TRAJECTORY: _____
    E. CONSISTENCY (PCT): _____
    F. FIELD GOAL RANGE: _____
    G. LONGEST FIELD GOAL: _____
    H. REACTION TO PRESSURE: _____
    _____
    _____
    _____

IX. **STATISTICS:** _____
    A. FG'S; FGM-FGA PCT 01-19 20-29 30-39 40-49 50+ LG BLK
    _____
    B. PAT'S: _____
X.   **KEY OBSERVATIONS:** _____
    _____
    _____
    _____
    _____
    _____
    _____

Diagram A-10b. A completed scouting (opponent) field goal/PAT team form.

SCOUTING (OPPONENT) FIELD GOAL/PAT TEAM

(97) K

(12) QB/WR

RB (37)   TE (84)   OL (71)   OL (69)   OC (6⊠8)   OL (50)   OL (73)   TE (44)   RB (34)

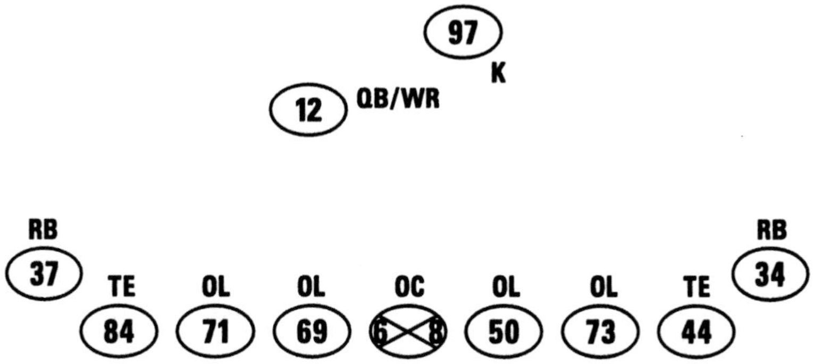

I. PROTECTION SCHEME:_____
   A. LINE: ⟍ Anchor inside _____
   B. ENDS: ⟋ _____
   C. WINGS: Double Bump _____
   * Balanced on the hash _____

II. A. STRENGTHS: _____
_____
_____
_____

   B. WEAKNESSES: _____
_____
_____
_____

III. HOLDER: _____ # 12
_____
   TEE IS PLACED: (7 yds.) _____

IV. SNAPPER: _____ (SR/SN) #68
_____

V. WINGS ELIGIBLE? Yes _____
VI. ENDS ELIGIBLE? Yes _____
VII. HOW DO WE BLOCK? _____

VIII. KICKER: _____ # 97
   A. (RT)/LT FOOTED: _____
   B. STEPS: _____
   C. GET OFF TIME: _____
   D. KICK TRAJECTORY: _____
   E. CONSISTENCY (PCT): #97-83%; #90-50%
   F. FIELD GOAL RANGE: _____
   G. LONGEST FIELD GOAL: _____
   H. REACTION TO PRESSURE: _____
   * #90 was Kicker earlier. # 97 has improved
     their FG game and long range!

IX. STATISTICS: _____

A. FG'S; FGM-FGA PCT 01-19 20-29 30-39 40-49 50+ LG BLK

	FGM-FGA	PCT	01-19	20-29	30-39	40-49	50+	LG	BLK
#97	5-6	83	0-0	2-2	3-4	0-0	0-0	38	0
#90	2-4	50	0-0	0-0	2-2	0-1	0-1	35	0

B. PAT'S: 17-20

X. KEY OBSERVATIONS: _____
   * Have attempted 2 Fakes. *See training tape*

   1. Shifted: Holder to QB, delay penalty

   2. Snap to Holder: ran off RE & RW,
     failed to get 1st down

Diagram A-11a. A sample scouting (opponent) field goal/PAT block team form.

SCOUTING (OPPONENT) FIELD GOAL/PAT BLOCK TEAM

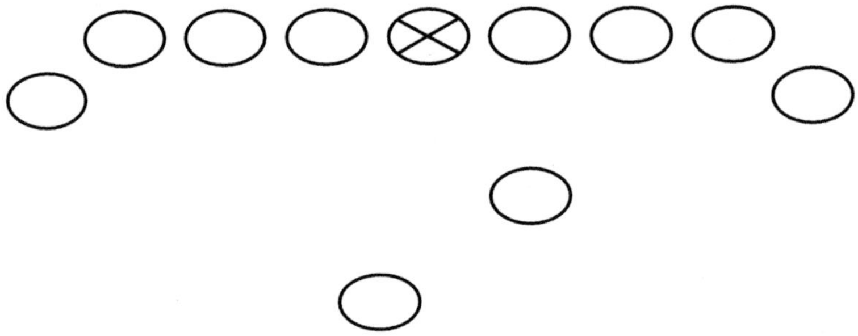

I. BLOCK SCHEME: _____

_____

_____

_____

_____

II. COVERAGE SCHEME: _____

_____

_____

_____

_____

III. BLOCKERS: NO: GAP:

_____ # _____ _____

_____ # _____ _____

_____ # _____ _____

_____ # _____ _____

_____ # _____ _____

_____ # _____ _____

IV. KEY OBSERVATIONS: _____

_____

_____

_____

_____

V. VULNERABLE TO FAKE? _____

_____

WHERE? _____

WHEN? _____

_____

HOW? _____

_____

VI. WHAT DEFENSIVE PERSONNEL? _____

_____

_____

_____

Diagram A-11b. A completed scouting (opponent) field goal/PAT block team form.

SCOUTING (OPPONENT) FIELD GOAL/PAT BLOCK TEAM

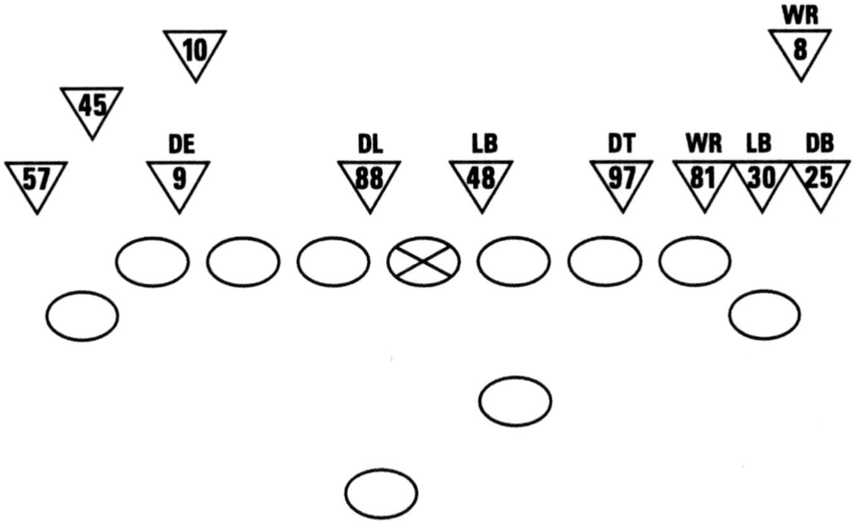

I. BLOCK SCHEME: _____
1. Outside RT
2. Outside LT
3. Middle Pinch with Jumpers

II. COVERAGE SCHEME: M/M

III. BLOCKERS:

	NO:	GAP:
_____	# 25	Outside RW
_____	# 45	Outside LW
_____	# ___	_____
_____	# 80	Inside Wing
_____	# ___	To blade side
_____	# ___	_____

IV. KEY OBSERVATIONS: _____
 Will usually outside block from
1. RT vs. PAT
2. Field vs. Has FG's

V. VULNERABLE TO FAKE? Yes

WHERE? To outside block side

WHEN? _____

HOW? _____

VI. WHAT DEFENSIVE PERSONNEL? Normal

Diagram A-12a. A sample scouting (opponent) PAT/FG blocks form.

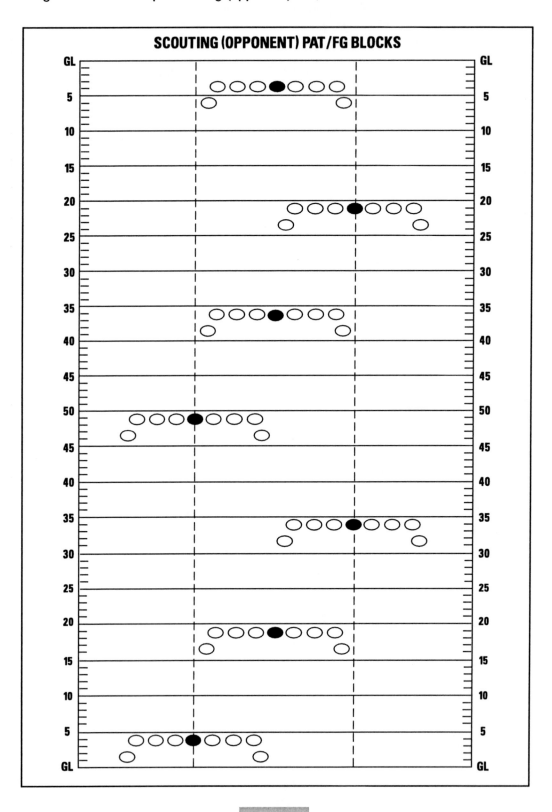

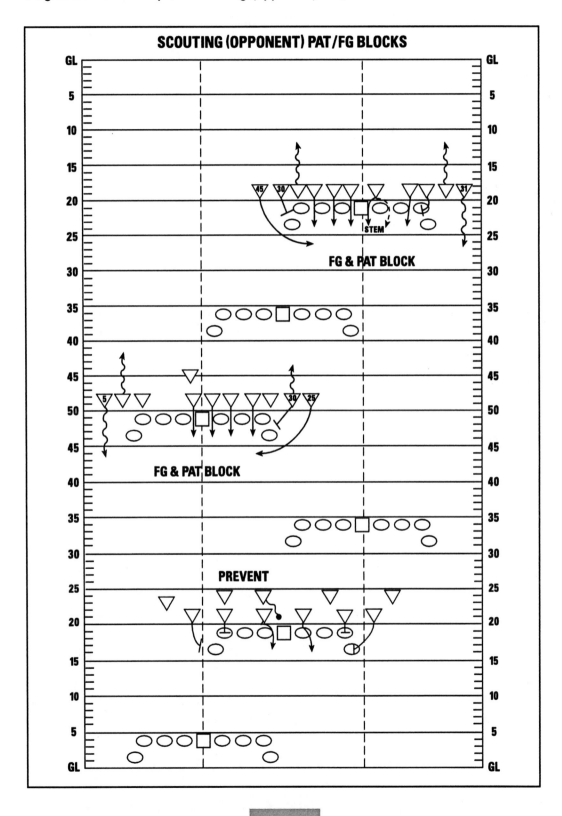

Dick Arbuckle has sixteen years of experience in the Pac 10 Conference, including fourteen years as a special teams coordinator. His most recent coaching assignment was at Arizona State for nine seasons as the tight ends and special teams coach. His resume includes nineteen years of experience as a head football coach on both the high school and college levels. After a successful high school coaching career in Oregon, he served as the head football coach at two different colleges in Oregon during the early 1980s. He guided Oregon Institute of Technology to a pair of league titles in 1981 and 1982, and was named Coach of the Year both seasons. He then moved to Western Oregon College.

Born in Los Angeles, Arbuckle graduated from the University of Oregon in 1961. He received a master's degree from Oregon in 1966.

During his undergraduate days, he was a two-year starter at safety for Oregon and played on the Duck's 1960 team, that earned a birth in the Liberty Bowl versus Penn State. He lettered in football, basketball and baseball while at El Monte High in Southern California, and earned All-CIF honors as a senior quarterback.

At the interscholastic level, Arbuckle earned a reputation for developing fine talent while a prep coach at Sheldon High School. Among his players who advanced to NFL careers were quarterback Chris Miller, tight end Todd Christensen, linebacker Mike Walter, and defensive back Jon Joqua.

He and his wife, Sherry, have three children, Vicki, Becki, and Joe, and five grandchildren.

Chuck Mottley has coached football at the intercollegiate, high school, and Pop Warner levels. He runs an annual kicking camp in Scottsdale, Arizona. Through the 1999 season, he served as a volunteer special teams coach at Chaparral (AZ) High School. The author of six books, including *Leadership in Action* with renowned coach, Bruce Snyder, he was a four-sport athlete in high school and a three-sport letterman in college.

In addition to being in the mining business for almost 40 years, Chuck has also been a political columnist. He and his wife, Linda, reside in Scottsdale, Arizona.